THE GOSPEL BLIMP

and other Modern Parables

JOSEPH BAYLY

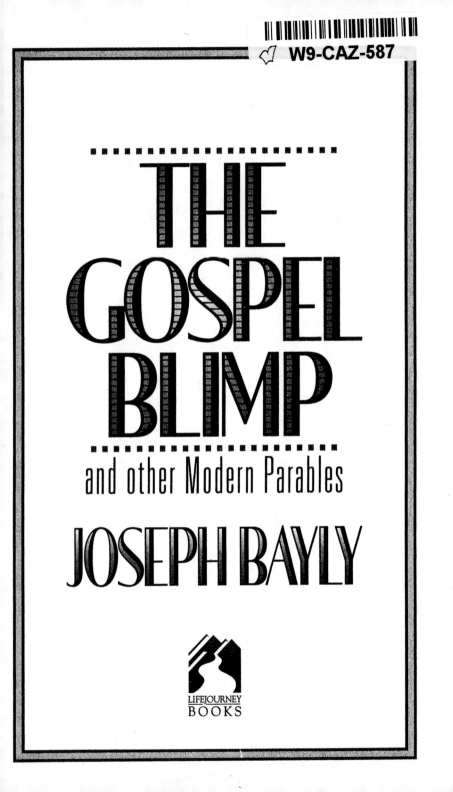

LIFEJOURNEY
BOOKS

To Mary Lou—
best friend,
encourager, and critic
for forty years.

The Gospel Blimp and Other Stories

Originally published in two volumes: *The Gospel Blimp.*
© 1960 by Joseph Bayly, and *How Silently, How Silently.*
© 1968, 1973 by Joseph Bayly.

David C. Cook Publishing Co., Elgin, IL 60120
David C. Cook Publishing Co., Weston, Ontario
Nova Distribution, Ltd., Newton Abbot, England

Cover design by Koechel, Peterson and Associates, Inc.

96 95 94 93 92 6 5 4 3 2

ISBN: 0-7814-0935-7
LC: 83-70533

Contents

The Gospel Blimp

Gooley and Friends

Meek Souls and Phonies

Afterword

The Gospel
Blimp

ONE

Conception of an Idea

THE IDEA REALLY BEGAN that night several years ago when we were all sitting around in George and Ethel Griscom's backyard.

We'd just finished eating an outdoor picnic supper (a real spread), and there wasn't much to do except swat mosquitoes and watch the fireflies. Every so often an airplane flew over, high in the sky. You could see the twinkling red and white lights.

I guess that's what got us started on the Gospel Blimp. Or maybe it was George and Ethel's next-door neighbors, who were playing cards and drinking beer on the porch.

Anyway we began talking about how to reach people with the gospel. Herm's active in the local businessmen's group (he and Marge were there that night, their first time out after the baby was born). So when we started talking about reaching people, Herm says, "Let's take those folks next door to you, George, for example. You can tell they're not Christians. Now if we wanted to give them the gospel, how'd we—"

"Herm, for goodness' sake, keep your voice down,"

Marge interrupted. "D'you want them to hear you?"

"Herm's right, they're not Christians," George agreed. "Go to church—a liberal one—Christmas and Easter. But drink and play cards most other Sundays. Except the summer. In a few weeks they'll start going to the shore each weekend until Labor Day."

"OK now. Any suggestions?" Herm is a good discussion leader.

"Hey, look at that plane. It's really low. You can almost see the lights in the windows."

"Portholes. More potato chips, anyone?"

"Like I was saying, here's a test. How do we go about giving the gospel to those people over there?" And Herm motioned toward the house next door.

"Too bad that plane didn't carry a sign. They looked up from their card playing long enough to have read it if it had carried one."

"Hey, you know, you may have something there. Any of you seen those blimps with signs trailing on behind? you know, 'Drink Pepsi Cola', or 'Chevrolet Is First?' "

"Volkswagen sales are really increasing. I read the other day—"

"What I mean is this. Why not have a blimp with a Bible verse trailing—something like 'Believe on the Lord Jesus Christ, and thou shalt be saved?' "

"I can see it now. The world's first vertical blimp, straight up and down like that tree. Anchored by a sign."

"Stop making fun. We could get a shorter verse."

"Sounds like a terrific idea. Really terrific. Why, everybody would get the gospel at the same time."

"Everybody except blind people and children who aren't able to read."

"Nothing's perfect. Anyway it does sound terrific, like Marge said."

"How'd we go about it? And wouldn't it be awfully expensive? I mean, buying the blimp, and blowing it up, and everything."

"Hey, it's time for the 'Maxie Belden Show.' "

"Aw, who wants to watch TV on a night like this, stars and breeze and all? Well, if everybody else is going inside . . ."

I guess we'd have left it at that—just one of those crazy things you talk about when a group gets together for supper and the evening—if it hadn't been for Herm.

Like I said, Herm's a good organizer. (I mean, I said he's a good discussion leader. But he's a good organizer, too.)

So the next Thursday Herm brought the idea up at our weekly businessmen's luncheon. He asked to make an announcement, and then he began. You could tell he was excited.

"Look, we want to reach people. And I've got a proposal to make. As you can see, we're not reaching them with our luncheons—" Here he paused and looked around the room. I did too, and I guess everybody else did. Not that we needed to. The regulars were there: three preachers and sixteen businessmen, two of them retired. And, of course, there was old Mr. Jensen. He doesn't do much anymore, but he still owns about half the real estate around town. I mean, a lot of houses and buildings—not necessarily half. And all of them Christians—the men at the luncheon, that is."

Well, Herm summarized the Gospel Blimp idea. He really did a good job. You could just tell that different ones were getting excited as he talked. Nobody even started on their ice cream until he was through.

"And so I suggest," Herm ended, in a real loud

voice, "that we appoint a committee. Maybe it's for the birds. Maybe not. But anyway," and here he paused and looked around the room again, "we ought to be reaching people somehow."

He'd hardly sat down when old Mr. Jensen was on his feet, real excited.

"Herm," he said. "I'm all for it. One hundred and ten percent. 'Course, there'll be problems, but nothing ventured, nothing lost. I think you ought to be chairman of the committee, Herm. Young fellow like him has lots of spizzerinkum, Fred," he finished, with a wink at our president, Dr. Gottlieb.

That afternoon we were a little late ending the luncheon, but by the time we did, a committee had been formed, with Herm as chairman.

"All you fellows on the committee, stay behind a few minutes," Herm called out above the scraping of the chairs as we rose to go. "We'll have to settle on a meeting time. This'll take work—lots of it."

Two
Labor Pains

LOTS OF WORK. That was the understatement of the year—maybe of the century.

First off we found we'd have to incorporate, otherwise the businessmen's group would have been liable, or maybe us personally. Liable financially, that is.

That constitution was a bear. It took two trips to the state capital before we got it approved. But finally, there we were, International Gospel Blimps, Inc. (We made it blimps instead of blimp because someone suggested the idea might spread. And if it did, we'd be in on the ground floor. Then Herm said, well, if it did spread, or if it might, why not be sure we take care of all eventualities. Why not make it international right from the start? So we did.)

Next we got stationery and receipts printed up. Since we'd gotten incorporated as a nonprofit organization, we could include the line on the receipt about contributions being tax-deductible.

This took all our time, and I mean all our time, for the next couple of months. That summer my lawn looked like a jungle. Especially after that week of rain late in the summer.

I remember that third week in August, because it was Friday evening, and I had gone over to George Griscom's to decide on accounting procedures. Money had begun to come in, and we'd just opened a bank account. It was about nine-thirty, and we were coming along OK when someone knocked on the screen door.

George got up and went. I heard him thank whoever it was for mowing his lawn. Then they talked for a few more minutes, and the man went away. I heard him call out, "Sorry you can't come," as he went off the porch.

"I'm sure glad you got that screen door closed," I said, half serious. "This place is crawling with mosquitoes."

"Listen," George says, and I can tell something's on his mind, "that was my next-door neighbor. Remember the guy who was drinking beer and playing cards with his wife on the porch when you were over in June? The night we dreamed up this Gospel Blimp idea? He just invited me, that is, Ethel and me, to go down to the shore with them this weekend. Of course I told him we couldn't go. Tomorrow's the full committee meeting, and Sunday afternoon's the IGBI prayer meeting.

"But that's not what I'm getting at," George continued. "What I mean is this. Wouldn't it be tremendous if he'd be the first fruit of the blimp? Both of them, I mean. It would sort of put a seal on it all if they'd become Christians. After all, they were why we thought of it in the first place."

So before I left, Ethel came in, and the three of us had prayer together that their neighbors would be saved through the Gospel Blimp.

Somehow as I drove home through the darkness, there was a peaceful sense of rightness about the IGBI plan. Maybe I'd had it before, maybe not. But tonight I knew. This was for people. And people would be saved.

People like the Griscoms' next-door neighbors.

I've sometimes wondered whether we'd have started on the whole thing if we'd known at the very beginning all that was involved.

Not the money. I don't mean that. Like somebody once said (maybe it was that fellow who started missions in China), "Have faith, think big, and tell the people. You'll get the money." And we did. It really came rolling in.

We were able to get an article about the Gospel Blimp in a Christian magazine, and did that ever stir up interest. We followed it up with a big advertisement. Money came in from all over. Also requests for information, suggestions of verses to be used at the blimp's tail, offers of hangar space, offers of uniforms for the crew. All kinds of offers.

At first I handled the correspondence, until I got swamped so bad I couldn't see my way out (complicated by its being Christmas and the kids having the measles). Honest, I never knew so many Christians were sign painters or had had experience on navy blimps and ground crews. I answered twenty-six letters from sign painters and nineteen from navy blimp Christians (not counting about a hundred air force guys) before I gave up and handed the job over to Herm.

One old gentleman even wrote from Germany to say he'd be honored to give us technical advice. (Doc Gottlieb read it for me—it was in German.) Seems he'd served on the *Hindenburg*—missed its last trip because he'd fallen off a ladder the day before it left Frankfurt. He was willing to serve without compensation—only wanted his passage money across the Atlantic.

Like I said, the whole thing mushroomed like an

inverted pyramid until we just had to do something. It was wrecking my home. I was out every night, and the only time I saw the kids was at breakfast. Love in our home meant "A bowl of cereal, a glass of milk, and you." (That's the year we celebrated Christmas five days late. At least the tree didn't cost us anything.)

So Herm finally decided to give up his job at the meat packing plant and go into the Gospel Blimp full-time. It was a big decision for him to make, giving up a good job with security and a pension and relatively safe work. On the other hand, as he pointed out to us, there was no real security in the Gospel Blimp, even though it looked promising. But he was willing to take a step of faith if we were behind him.

And we were. Especially me, for reasons that should be obvious. I was about at the end of my rope.

THREE

The Blimp Is Delivered

THE BLIMP WAS DELIVERED in April. It drifted in, sort of lazylike, from the East, where it had been manufactured.

We were all on hand, plus about five hundred other people, to see it come down into the hangar. (Did I tell you old Mr. Jensen gave some ground just beyond the city limits, down near the sewage disposal plant, for the hangar?)

It was a beauty. I've never seen Herm so touched— said it made him think of a perfect sausage, a perfect one.

That night we had a sort of send-off dinner up at Second Church. Speeches by the mayor (that was before the time when persecution began), by the head of the ministerial associate (he, too, was extremely friendly still), and by a Christian navy commander.

Afterward we all got in our cars and drove out to the hangar, where the Gospel Blimp was christened. Herm's little girl broke a bottle of Seven-Up over it. (We originally thought of Coke, but someone suggested that seven is the number of perfection, so we used Seven-Up.)

George Griscom invited us over to his house afterward—everybody who'd been there that night we had the original idea for the blimp, almost a year ago. We were sort of sober, thinking of all that lay ahead.

"You know," George said, "if only my next-door neighbors are saved. If they are, it'll be worthwhile. All the work and money and time."

"Listen," Herm said, "it can't fail. They can read, can't they? Well, tomorrow morning at eight sharp they'll see the gospel in the sky. Right over their house. I promise you, George, in my capacity as general director of International Gospel Blimps, Incorporated. And not just your next-door neighbors. The whole block. My block. Every block in the city. Every last one. But we'll start with your block, George. Seems only right, doesn't it?" And he looked around the room for approval.

We all nodded or said yes, it sure did.

"What verse are you starting out with, Herm?"

"That would be telling. You'll see tomorrow morning, bright and early. Well, everybody, guess we'd better call it a night."

Next morning I drove past George's house on my way to work, starting a little early so I'd get there just at eight. Sure enough, there was the blimp. And trailing on behind was the sign. It was really beautiful, with the early morning sun highlighting those bold red letters.

Why, the gospel could be seen for blocks!

Maybe it was too early in the day, but I didn't see anyone out looking up at it. So after stopping the car for a minute across from George's house, I went on to work.

I went out for lunch that day (often I'd bring it in a bag, and just get a cup of coffee at the soda fountain on the first floor). But I went out, and first thing I did was look up between the buildings at the sky. No blimp.

So I walked several blocks to this little sandwich shop some of us go to, hoping I'd run into one or two of the fellows. Sure enough, George and a couple of others were there.

"Seen the blimp?" George asked me.

"First thing this morning, on my way to work."

"Boy, is it beautiful. You can see that sign almost a mile off."

"Wonder where it is now. Herm should have brought it downtown for the lunch hour."

"Well, there's going to be a lot of lunch hours before we're finished with that bag."

We didn't know it then, but we were almost finished with the blimp right at that moment. In fact, we found out later that's the reason Herm didn't have it downtown for the noon hour.

Seems Herm and the other guy (this graduate of a Christian flying school we had hired) were cruising along just over the rooftops, when there was this tremendous jolt, followed by a hissing sound. Next thing they knew they were losing altitude, but fast.

Must have been a frightening experience. (Herm said later he expected the whole thing to go thrrp-l-p-ssss the way a balloon does when you blow it up and release it in the air without tying it, that is, the end you blow into. But it didn't.) In a few minutes they came to rest, sort of wedged between two houses.

I wish I'd been there to see those two women come running out of their front doors. One of them had been making beds upstairs when suddenly all the light from the outside was extinguished. So she ran over to the window, threw it open, and there was this thing. It sort of gave when she pushed against it, and there was this hissing sound. Well, she ran screaming into the street.

The other lady called the fire department, and they soon had a hook-and-ladder truck there.

"I've gotten cats out of trees, and kids out of bathrooms, but this is the first time I've gotten two guys off a blimp," this fireman in charge of the truck said, according to Herm. Herm says he used some other language, too, which was the opportunity for a witness.

It took a few weeks to get the blimp back in shape again. Seems they were flying too low, and the pilot wasn't watching carefully the way he should have been. Besides, he wasn't yet familiar with our little city. The big thing he didn't know was that a radio station's tower was located plumb in the middle of this residential section. So first thing he'd ripped the blimp's bottom on the tower. But finally it was ready to return to the air. (I mean the blimp. The radio station's programs weren't interrupted. That was no factor in the later persecution.)

Four
Togetherness

Meanwhile we'd gotten prepared for the long haul. By that I mean we learned a lesson from that first day. This job wouldn't be done overnight. There would be opposition; the enemy had already tried to ruin the blimp.

So we started prayer meetings for the safety of the blimp and those whose lives would be constantly endangered by flying in it. These prayer meetings were held downtown each noon hour for those of us who could come, in the International Gospel Blimps, Inc., office. (I forgot to tell you we'd rented three rooms in the Bender Building.) Thursdays we didn't meet there, since that was the day of the businessmen's lunch. But we spent a good bit of time in prayer at the lunch, too.

The wives had their prayer meeting every Tuesday night. They combined their praying with work on these fire bombs, which they filled.

But I'm getting ahead of my story.

After the rip in the blimp was repaired, Herm got the thing running on a regular schedule. This was possible because we let this other fellow, the first one we had, go.

He was undependable, and besides he didn't know enough about flying, as witness the radio tower episode. But we really got a wonderful replacement who had spent four years flying navy blimps out of Lakehurst, New Jersey. He was a young married fellow who'd been considering the mission field. In fact, he'd applied for South America or Africa or someplace. But, with his wife's help, we finally convinced him that this was much more strategic, because look at all the kids and young people he could influence for missions with this job.

Just so I won't forget this part of the blimp's ministry, let me tell you that this new fellow wasn't with us very long before he convinced the board that we should have a missionary emphasis on the blimp. So we decided that every Saturday afternoon would be Missionary Blimp Afternoon. (We chose Saturday because we knew the Christian kids don't go to the movies then, like so many other kids.) We used missionary signs on the blimp and released junior missionary bombs.

I was interested to see how my own kids would be affected by this new missionary emphasis, especially because they'd sort of come to resent the time I (also their mother) was spending on blimp work. Maybe resent is too strong a word. It was more a matter of their saying, "Aw, another night out working on the blimp? You haven't been home since a week ago Saturday." They also were rather bitter about what happened at the football game.

Anyway, I was really happy when this one Sunday on the way home from church my boy brought up the subject. He said he'd been thinking about the blimp, and the missionary sign the blimp had pulled the afternoon before (it was, I believe, the One Billion Unreached one).

As a result of all this thinking, he said, "I've decided to learn to pilot a blimp when I grow up. I'm going to enlist in the navy."

"It's not fair," says his little sister. "It's really not fair at all. Boys get to do everything. I could never be a missionary. Girls don't get to learn to fly blimps. All they get to do is play with dolls and wash the bathroom floor and—" She stopped for breath.

"Huh," says our oldest girl, the one who's in high school. "Who'd want to have anything to do with a blimp, anyway? Only a creep. A real, square creep. Brother, I mean, that Gospel Blimp is—"

"Judy, be careful of your mouth," her mother warns her. "It can get you in trouble."

"Trouble? What do you call what I and the other Christian kids got in over what happened at the game with Central? I guess the blimp had nothing to do with that. My mouth didn't get us into that trouble. There we were, ahead at the half, and then that darn blimp has to come along and—"

"Judy, that will be enough. You may set the table when we get home."

"Besides," I felt constrained to add in the blimp's defense, "everyone agrees that it was one of those freak accidents. One chance in a million of its happening. You can't really blame the blimp."

I think I told you about the fire bombs we were using. We named them that because they represented revival fire falling on the unsaved.

The IGBI Women's Auxiliary fixed them, like I said, at their weekly meetings. There wasn't really much to making them—they just took a tract and wrapped it up in different colored cellophane. There were loose ends sticking out, so that when they were dumped overboard from the blimp, they sort of floated to earth.

At first the kids chased them all over—I hear someone spread the rumor that there was bubble gum in them. But after a couple of days, no one got particularly excited when they fell.

The Commander (Herm wanted us to call him that now) made quite an affair out of dumping the load, according to the blimp pilot.

"Bombs away!" he'd shout, and then he'd shoot them down, alternating colors (each color was a different tract).

And always, when he'd have a new tract, he'd try to dump some on George Griscom's next-door neighbor's lawn. He wasn't forgetting, the Commander wasn't, our covenant with George about his neighbor.

Not that there was any encouragement along that line. Once, I recall, I stopped at Griscoms' to return George's power drill. I'd been getting the PA system ready to install on the blimp. So I asked Ethel about their neighbors.

"Nothing new," she says. "I mean, nothing to get excited about as far as their salvation is concerned. But she hasn't been well. I think they took her to the hospital two or three days ago. We can see him eating over there alone at night. And always a bottle of beer. Sometimes two."

"What hospital's she in?" I asked.

"I don't know. I'll tell George you stopped with the drill. By the way, how's the sound system coming?"

"Oh, some bugs yet. But give us a few more nights like tonight and we'll be ready to roll."

"Will people really be able to hear it?"

"With a hundred-watt output? And three cone

speakers? Listen, they'll be able to hear it anywhere—even in a basement. No worry about that."

"The Women's Auxiliary is really thrilled about the sound system. You know, we've been concerned about blind people, and children who can't read yet, and people who are nearsighted. And people who can't get outside to see the blimp, like invalids, and old men and women in convalescent homes, and people in hospitals. It'll be comforting to know we're doing something for them."

"Well, tell George I stopped. And thanks for the drill."

FIVE
A Small Cloud

WHEN WE STARTED USING the PA system about a week later, a new epoch in the Gospel Blimp's ministry began. In a sense, it seemed to give final assurance that the total evangelization of our little city was a distinct possibility.

But it also marked the beginning of the period of active opposition. Forces were unleashed that we hardly knew existed beneath the calm surface of life all around us.

I'll never forget that first night. I had gone down to the drugstore to get a box of candy and a card (having been reminded during dessert that it was our wedding anniversary), when suddenly I heard it.

In loud tones, on the wings of the night, as it were, came the sound of "Rolled away, rolled away, rolled away, every burden of my heart rolled away." Honest, it was tremendous.

People came out of houses, cars stopped, everybody tried to figure where it was coming from.

Of course I knew. For I had put the last Phillips screw through the third speaker only that afternoon. But the rest of the people were puzzled because the blimp was nowhere in sight.

Next came the vibraharp rendition of the "Glory Song," followed by about fifty kids singing the "Hash Chorus." But it wasn't until the music had stopped, and the Commander's voice came on, "Now hear this, all you people," that the blimp hovered into sight. It wasn't a full moon, but it was still bright enough to see the blimp clearly outlined against the sky.

I suppose the Commander preached about ten minutes that first time. Or maybe it took ten minutes for the blimp to get out of earshot. But even though it was short, he was able to get in two invitations. The vibraharp came on for a few bars of "Almost Persuaded" each time. (I should explain that the music was recorded on tape, although Herm's messages were live. It was only later that he taped the full program, including his own preaching. But that was while he was out of town.)

I tell you, I was really thrilled. When I got home with the candy, I phoned up the Griscoms to tell them the good news.

"I know why you're calling" says George before I have a chance to tell him. "Listen." And he holds the phone away from his head. In the background, coming through clear as a bell, I can hear, "Hallelu, Hallelu, Hallelu."

Were we ever enthused! I think, looking back, that night was the high point of the whole blimp project. But we were totally unprepared for the next morning.

I picked up the *Trib* on my way to the office. And there on the front page, down toward the bottom, was a story about the "airborne sound truck." It was the first time the blimp had hit the papers. (Earlier there had been a few lines about the christening, and a notice of the public meeting, but nothing like this.)

I guess I must have been sort of walking on air when I came into the office. Of course the guys I work with had known for a long time about my interest in the blimp. But they had sort of treated it something like— well, like the guy who bowls every night, or the fellow who's a scoutmaster. So now they could see the significance of my project, and they had probably even heard the gospel the night before.

Anyway, I sort of remarked casual-like after I'd hung up my coat, "You fellows see the newspaper story on the blimp?"

"Which one?"

"Why, there is only one," I say. "You know, the one I'm interested in, the gospel one."

"No, I mean which story? There are two, or didn't you know?"

"Where's the other one? I only saw the one on the front page." And suddenly I'm sort of sorry I brought up the subject, because everybody's quiet, and nobody's smiling.

"Well, then, maybe you'd better read the one on the editorial page, Buster."

So I sat down at my desk and read it. It was an editorial entitled "The Right to Peace." And it began— here, I have a copy—

> *For some weeks now our metropolis has been treated to the spectacle of a blimp with an advertising sign attached at the rear. This sign does not plug cigarettes, or a bottled beverage, but the religious beliefs of a particular group in our midst. The people of our city are notably broadminded, and they have good-naturedly submitted to this attempt to proselyte. But last night a new*

refinement (some would say debasement) was
introduced. We refer, of course, to the airborne
sound truck, that invader of our privacy, that
raucous destroyer of communal peace. That the
voices of some of our city's beloved schoolchildren
were used does not take away from . . .

Well, that's enough for you to get the general drift.

It seemed as if lunch would never come. When it did, I hurried over to the place I mentioned before, even though I'd brought my lunch. I mean the lunchroom where the Christian fellows often eat.

As soon as I saw them I knew we'd all had the same experience.

We talked it over, including all the angles. And when it came time for us to get back to work, someone—maybe it was George—seemed to sum it up when he said, "Well, we were told we'd be persecuted for righteousness' sake and I guess this is it. So we'll just have to stand together, foursquare."

That night our IGBI board of directors held an emergency meeting downtown to discuss the situation. We'd hardly gotten started, when the phone rang. It was the pilot—he'd just returned from supper to take the blimp out for its final run of the day. When he got inside the hangar, he found someone had broken in and sabotaged the blimp's PA system. Nothing else was touched.

The Commander told him to lock up and go on home for the night, and not to talk to anybody about what had happened. Then we settled down to discuss what to do. Somehow it seemed a much more pressing matter than it had before the phone call.

When we broke up around midnight, we'd come to

certain decisions. In the first place, we decided that we'd
continue to use the PA system on the blimp, no matter
what happened. But we'd turn down the volume a bit.
Next, we'd see if we couldn't get the sign electrified so
that people could see where the sound was coming from
when we broadcast at night. And finally, on the
Commander's recommendation, we decided to hire a
public relations man who'd be responsible for keeping the
blimp in good with the general public. The Commander
also said such a man could get money from Christians to
pay for the blimp and the salaries and the sound system
and the office and everything else.

The whole operation was costing about five thousand dollars per month, and even with contributions
coming in from all over the country, it was still a strain.
So we gladly voted to accept Herm's recommendation. I
might even say that we breathed a sigh of relief. At least
I did, because we were in a whole lot deeper than we
ever imagined we'd be that Thursday afternoon about
ten months ago, when Herm first brought the blimp up
at our businessmen's lunch.

SIX
Architect of Goodwill

THAT NEW PUBLIC RELATIONS fellow really knew his business. First thing he did was arrange a big dinner—to recoup our forces and make new friends, he said. The IBGI Women's Auxiliary worked on it, and it was really well planned. Ham and sweets and everything else, with ice cream blimp molds for dessert. For favors they had little blimp banks—to save up money so you could pay your pledge, that is, if you made one. The whole dinner was gratis—there were no tickets and no offering. Just the opportunity to pledge at the end.

It was a bit disappointing that some of the people we invited didn't come. The mayor declined because of a previous engagement, and he was also too busy to write us a letter to be read at the dinner.

But the dinner was just the beginning of this public relations fellow's activity. As he expressed it, "Any item of interest about the blimp or its ministry is legitimate news. And new builds goodwill."

So he got little items in the papers about how much helium the blimp contained and where the helium came from, about the Commander moving to his new house, about the church affiliations of members of board, about the women's Auxiliary luncheons and parties, about the electric generating plant on the blimp, about all sorts of other things. One or two of these items even made the radio news summary.

He also had a regular news service for Christian magazines with plenty of photographs. Pictures of the Commander releasing the one millionth fire bomb were published by about ten different periodicals. Another time a picture of the Commander at the wheel made the front cover of a big Christian magazine.

This public relations fellow was working on the theory that International Gospel Blimps was too impersonal. People couldn't feel "empathy," as he put it, with a nonprofit corporation, or even with a blimp. Too big and fat and cold. So more and more he built up the Commander as the blimp's personification. He got the Commander to grow a beard (like those guys in the magazine advertisements), and also to wear a new uniform. The old one was something like a policeman's, but the new one was beautiful, Powder blue, with shiny gold buttons and gold stripes on the sleeves. That visor had enough braid on it for an admiral.

The Commander was spending less and less time on the blimp. At our new public relations man's suggestion he joined the best golf club, so he could meet the people whose influence really counts, and who could contribute substantially to IGBI. He also began taking speaking engagements all over—not just churches, but service clubs and women's clubs and other meetings of that sort.

That summer he wasn't around much, because he had a full schedule of engagements at Bible conferences. Sometimes he took Marge with him, but mostly he'd just go off in his Mercedes-Benz alone.

I'm told he had quite a ministry at these conferences, especially in terms of getting young people to dedicate their lives to Christian service. He talked a lot about sacrifice, and told about how he'd given up a successful career in business when he felt the call. No holding back, no looking around from the plow. Straight ahead, whatever the cost.

And the money really came in. There was no doubt about that public relations fellow knowing what he was doing.

Funny thing happened about this time. The Commander was leaving on one of his trips this particular Thursday afternoon, and he came to the businessmen's luncheon first. He wasn't able to come very often anymore, so we were all glad to see him.

Herm gave a report, and then we reminisced some, recalling how enthusiastic old Mr. Jensen (the one who gave us the land on which the hangar was placed) had been that first time we ever discussed the blimp. Most of us had been at Mr. Jensen's funeral a few weeks before. (Incidentally he left $5,000 in his will to IGBI, some to the Commander, too, in view of his sacrifice.)

Anyway, after the meeting, while Herm got in the driver's seat, we told him we'd loaded the bombs for him to drop on his trip. As far as we were concerned it was just a practical joke. We were all standing around ready to empty the bombs back into the basket and take them away.

But Herm didn't take it as a joke. He sort of froze, didn't even say good-bye, and drove off. Later we found them dumped on the ground out near the hangar.

SEVEN
Cloudburst

THAT FALL EVERYTHING was going fine, and all of us had sort of settled down to the kind of life we'd known before the blimp came along.

The blimp was on a regular schedule, flying all over the city during the daytime, concentrating on shopping centers and special events at night. People had come to accept the blimp—fact is, there was a sort of community pride of ownership. No other place had a Gospel Blimp, you know, although a lot of them had expressed interest.

Opposition to the blimp had all but died out, largely as a result of turning down the volume on the PA system and the public relations work.

There was one new development: foreign language programs. Although they weren't large, our city had several foreign sections. These included Chinatown, Italian and Polish communities, and one suburb that was largely German. So we rigged up signs in these languages and also recorded foreign language programs on tape. Then we had regular days and nights during the month when the blimp concentrated on each of these foreign groups.

It was one of these nights, the Polish one, when all the goodwill Herm and the public relations fellow had been building up came crashing around us. And not just the non-Christians; Christians were screaming for our hides just as loudly.

That Tuesday evening began in our home about the same as it did in thousands of other homes, I guess. We'd finished supper and the kids were hurrying to get the dishes done so they wouldn't miss any of the television programs. Tuesday night was, of course, the best night on TV. That was our downfall.

Let me explain at this point that the Gospel Blimp took to the air about seven o'clock that night. Everything was shipshape: the Polish sign was already lighted up, the baskets were full of fire bombs, the tape recorder was loaded and ready to roll with a completely Polish program. Everything was shipshape with one exception. But we couldn't have known ahead of time. Even the Federal Communications Commission later admitted that at the public hearing.

At any rate, we had just settled down in front of the TV set to watch "Pistol Bark," when the sound sort of fades and instead of hearing what's happening on the program, we're listening to some sort of foreign gibberish.

"Hey, what's happening?" I ask. "Turn it to some other channel and let's see if it's just on the one station."

One station, every station: the same foreign language program.

"Boy, is some radio station going to get it in the neck for this blooper," I say.

And then it happens. The speaking ends and a vibraharp rendition of "Sunshine, Sunshine, in My Soul Today" begins. Four verses.

A guy gets pumped full of lead, lips move, a horse

gallops away. But no sound. Just "Sunshine, Sunshine, in My Soul Today."

The program ends, and little cigarettes march around on the screen, out of step, to the tune of "Sunshine, Sunshine, in My Soul Today."

By this time I'm on the phone, and so are fifty thousand other people. I wait and wait for the dial tone and finally give up.

Besides, what can I do? What can anyone do?

Next comes the "Maxie Belden Show," the most popular program on TV—or at least it was then. Maxie comes on with a great big smile and begins talking Polish. This girl with the low-cut dress sings, only her voice is bass, and the words are "Dwelling in Beulah Land." In Polish. It was horrible. I can't describe how I felt.

My oldest girl, the one in high school begins to cry.

"What's the matter?" I ask. "Don't take it so hard. You can see what's going on even if you can't hear it."

"It's not that," she sobs. And then she lets out a real wail. "What am I going to say tomorrow at school? This is awful—much awfuller than what happened at the game with Central. Oh, that darn, horrible blimp." And she runs upstairs to her room.

"Maybe," I suggest, but without much conviction, "maybe it's not on all the TV sets. Maybe ours is an exception."

But just a few seconds later any lingering, hopeful doubts were dissipated by the sign. It was printed rather crudely. I guess by the local station engineer: "Due to circumstances beyond our control, interference prevents listeners in this area from receiving sound on this or any other channel. Steps are being taken to correct this situation. Meanwhile, keep tuned to this station."

Just then the phone rings. George Griscom is really upset. He's been trying to get hold of the Commander but he's out of town. Marge doesn't know where he is, except that he left early this afternoon.

"What are we going to do?" George practically shouts over the phone. "Every minute that goes by, our stock gets lower with people. Maybe they'll even tar and feather us—I wouldn't put it past them. Not when you interfere with the 'Maxie Belden Show.' "

"Nothing we can do." I admit. "After all, there's no telephone connection to the blimp. Let's see, it's about eight-thirty now. He's due to stay up there another two hours, maybe longer on a clear night like this."

"What in the world's causing it? The TV interference, I mean."

"I'm not sure, but somehow or other the blimps amplifier is broadcasting on television frequency. It shouldn't really be transmitting at all, but it is. And it's a freak that the picture is okay. I'd expect it to go with the sound."

"Maybe we could build a big fire or something," George suggests in a hopeless sort of any-port-in-a-storm tone of voice.

"How'd he know we meant him? And how'd we get him to bring the blimp down?"

Every television station in town had the same idea, though. Before long we heard guns and rockets going off. But who up in a blimp is going to think they're trying to attract his attention? It's just a big celebration in town that he didn't know about. Maybe, since it seems to be mainly localized beneath him, it's a Polish holiday.

And even when some private planes begin to buzz the blimp, it doesn't mean anything to him. Just crazy pilots, having some sort of drag race, using the blimp as their turning mark.

The one man who could have changed the situation in a moment was the one man who was totally unaware that anything was happening. Just the flip of a switch and peace would have flooded the community. But he didn't know. And so for two more hours the switch was left unflipped. Vibraharp, ten-minute sermon, invitation, "Almost Persuaded," hymn or chorus, vibraharp, on and on, around and around. Everything in Polish except the vibraharp.

And it came out here, on TV. Every channel, every set.

Some people called it a night and went to bed about nine-thirty, we found out later. They were in the happiest frame of mind, relatively speaking, next day.

Like I said earlier, it was a clear night. So the pilot kept going until about ten to eleven. Then he turned off the lights and the PA system and headed back to the hangar, blissfully unaware of what awaited him there.

He said later that he wondered why the big crowd. But he sure found out soon enough after he'd maneuvered the blimp into the hangar.

First were the police, with a summons for disturbing the peace. Then the reporters and photographers. And everywhere the crowd of people, raving mad, some of them shouting, "Let us have the bum! Burn the blimp!"

And in the background, waiting around until the police dispersed the crowd, were the board members of International Gospel Blimps, Inc.

Somehow or other, I think all of us realized that night was the beginning of the end. The end of the blimp as we had known it, the Gospel Blimp, which had come into our lives and filled them and crowded out almost everything else.

The wonderful, shiny blimp. The "darn" blimp to use my oldest girl's usual description. The blimp that had its origin almost two years ago, that summer evening in George Griscom's backyard.

I look over at George, sitting on a box by the fence, waiting. Good old George, so faithful all these months to the blimp and its ministry. George and Ethel, so anxious for their next-door neighbors to be saved through the Gospel Blimp. Here the end is in sight, and they're not yet saved. All that praying for them, and they're not saved. All those special trips the blimp has made, flying low over their house, PA blaring away, fire bombs dropping. And they're not yet Christians. No wonder George looks so discouraged, sitting over there.

It seems forever, but finally the police get the crowd cleared away from the hangar and the people begin to get in their cars. A little group has found a basket of fire bombs, and they're standing around the fire it makes in the middle of the field. But even that group is beginning to joke, and seems to be getting in a better mood. For one thing, the pilot's reaction was so honest when he found out what happened that the crowd had to laugh.

"Think we'll post a couple of men here for the night, just in case," the police lieutenant says to the pilot. "Never can tell. Not that I'd mind, particularly. Not after what happened to the "Maxie Belden Show" and getting that emergency call out here when I was all comfortable at home. But duty's duty. Want an officer to drive home with you, just in case?"

"No," says the pilot. "I've got to see some friends first anyway—the Gospel Blimp board members. That's them over there. I guess we'll have a lot of talking to do."

"Well, call your precinct if you need us during the

night. Think I'll get on home to the late-late show. And by the way, I think I'd keep that thing in the hangar the next few days."

"Thanks for the advice. Also for the help earlier. I thought for a while they might be thinking about lynching me, or at least they'd throw me in the sedimentation pool at the sewage disposal plant over there."

"You were lucky, my friend. But don't push it. 'Night." And the lieutenant swung into the police car.

"Hi, fellows," the pilot says to us as we close in on him. "Where's Herm? Where'll we go to talk? I want to sit down, wherever it is. I don't know about you guys, but I've just had a tough two hours. For a while there I was wishing I was out on the mission field."

"We," George says firmly, with emphasis, "we've had a tough five hours. Almost six."

"Well, don't blame it on me," says the pilot. "I was only the pilot. I never claimed to be an electrical engineer. Besides, it was me almost got tossed in with the sewage. Let's get away from here. This place gives me the creeps."

So we went over to George's place. Ethel fixed egg sandwiches and coffee for us. We didn't stay long though—only about an hour. There wasn't much we could decide, what with Herm not being there and all.

But we did have some prayer about the situation before breaking up. And we remembered to pray for George and Ethel's next-door neighbors. Ethel suggested that we should.

EIGHT
Truth Is Organized

HERM GOT BACK NEXT day around noon. First thing he did after finding he'd backed into a hornet's nest was get together with the public relations fellow.

What they came up with wasn't what the rest of us expected, but you could see that it was only reasonable. Or at least we came to see that it was after they explained it to us. Our first reaction on seeing the evening newspapers, I'll admit, wasn't good.

What they did was this. The public relations man drew up a statement, which Herm signed, and copies were taken to all the papers and radio and television stations.

In this statement Herm first apologized to the public for the inconvenience caused by the "irresponsible actions" of International Gospel Blimps. He next expressed regret that he had been out of town on business the previous evening, when these irresponsible actions had come to such an unfortunate climax. Then he said how if he had been here it would never have happened. (I never could understand that part of his statement. After all, Herm knows nothing about electronics.) But now that he was back again, he promised the public that he personally would see to it that there would be no repetition of the previous night's "fiasco." And, further, he wanted to assure our city that he would see to it that "any irresponsible element" in IGBI was dropped, and that this great community project would have "increasing civic consciousness." Finally, he appealed to the public for their sympathetic understanding of the tremendous pressures under which he had been working.

Well, that's about what Herm's statement said.

That night the board met in a special emergency session. All of us had read the statement in the papers, or heard it over television or radio. So we were sort of quiet when we came together down at IGBI headquarters.

"Hi, fellows," Herm says when he comes in with the public relations fellow, about a half hour late. "What's everyone so solemn for? You'd think you'd lost your best friend or something. Cheer up, everything's settled. We've got it made. Haven't we?" he asks, turning to the public relations fellow.

"Sure have, Commander," he replies.

I guess this was too much for George Griscom. So he begins, "About that statement you gave to the papers, Herm—"

"Oh, that. Just to quiet people down. Really nothing to it, nothing more than that. You know how it is. We've been in this thing from the beginning, and we've weathered a lot of storms together. Good ship. Good fellowship. Nothing to it."

"Commander, could I put in a word?" asks the public relations fellow.

"Sure thing. Only hurry—I want to get this meeting over with. Big day tomorrow."

"I'd like to explain why we issued that statement.

You see, like I've told you before, it's hard to sell an idea. It's easier to sell a man. It's hard to sell a corporation, nonprofit or regular. It's much easier to sell an individual—especially a guy like the Commander. You all know that.

"Well, once you've sold people on somebody as representing the idea or the movement," he continues, "you have to see that they never lose confidence in him. They can lose confidence in the idea, they can lose confidence in the corporation. With all due respect to you men, they can even lose confidence in the members of the board.

"But there's one person," he concludes, pointing his finger at us, "they can't lose confidence in. That's the man you've built up as a symbol. In the case of IGBI, that's the Commander."

Everything's quiet for a minute or two. Then George Griscom asks, only he's not really asking, "So you decide to sell the rest of us down the river."

"Of course not," Herm interrupts before the public relations fellow has a chance to reply. "Of course not. That's not fair, George, if you don't mind my saying so. All it amounts to is this. Which is more important: you or the blimp? If you had to chose, which would it be: your membership on the board, or the success of this Gospel Blimp project? After all, George, you must remember that you have a great deal more at stake than many others. It's your next-door neighbors we've given special attention to. I've asked for no special thanks from you for all I've done. Fact is, I've sacrificed a great deal without much appreciation. But then when something like this comes along, you can hardly blame me for wanting to see just a bit of loyalty from you fellows."

George sort of has a hangdog expression.

"Actually it was a godsend that the Commander was out of town last night during the television incident," the public relations man continues. "If he'd been here, everybody would have known that he could do no more than anyone else to correct the situation. And the net result would have been a loss of public confidence in him. That would have been disastrous. A man in his position, like I said, may have feet of clay, but we've got to hide them from the public.

"The question isn't whether the Commander could or couldn't have done anything about the mess if he'd been here at the time it happened. It's that we can't let people know he couldn't. We've got to preserve their image of the Commander as a man who is in complete control of every situation."

"Would you lie to do that?" George says it real soft.

"That's a nasty word," the Commander says, looking straight at George. "And it's hardly a Christian attitude toward someone who's done as much for the Gospel Blimp as he has," putting his arm around the public relations fellow's shoulder.

"I guess there isn't much more to discuss, is there?" someone remarks, standing up.

"Just this," the Commander says. "Sit down a minute. Any of you guys don't like the way I'm running things, then, if you don't, why, for the sake of our harmony and testimony as a Christian organization, I think you ought to drop off the board. Nobody is indispensable."

"Except Herm," George murmurs close by my ear. "Nobody but Herm."

That was the last board meeting George ever attended. He just sort of dropped out. It made us all feel bad, but after all, there was a lot to be done. And personal feelings had to be subordinated to the Gospel Blimp. This was no time for discord. It was a time for pitching in, for rolling up our sleeves, for putting our heads to the grindstone.

The blimp weathered the storm with only one casualty: the PA system. We had to agree to drop that in order to satisfy the FCC, the City Council, and public opinion. Also, most of the Christians. Nobody wanted a repeat of the Maxie Belden incident.

So we settled down to the long haul. None of us on the IGBI board had quite the same feelings as we'd had earlier. But we decided that we'd put these things out of our mind for the blimp's sake.

Same way with Herm's family trouble. When we heard that he wasn't living at home any longer, and why he'd been taking those trips out of town, that really knocked us for a loop, temporarily. But after discussing it a long time (the meeting didn't end until three a.m.), with Herm not in on the discussion, we decided to give him the benefit of the doubt. Besides, as somebody said, Herm had really given himself to this project, right from the very start. Who else would have had the faith to take such a step as giving up his job at the meat packing plant?

After Marge actually filed for divorce, the issue became a lot bigger. For a while I thought it would split the board, but we were able to hold things together for the sake of the blimp. Our only loss was the blimp's pilot. He resigned after trying to get the board to do something about Herm. But there were plenty of Christian pilots around, and we got a good one.

As for Herm, he was spending more and more time in public relations work. By now he was in good with most of the civic and business leaders of our city. This brought in a fair amount of income, including grants from several foundations. (But it was still the thousands of little people, Christians, whose regular gifts paid the bills.)

NINE
Autumn Flight

ONE PLACE THAT HERM cultivated these important people was at the country club. He liked to play golf and these executives seemed to like having him around.

The issue that really threatened to split our IGBI board began, innocently enough, on the golf course.

Herm had given orders to the blimp pilot that he wasn't to fly over the country club. The distraction bothered people who were playing, Herm said, and besides, since he—the Commander—was there so much, the blimp really wasn't needed. And, of course, the pilot obeyed his instructions.

This one day, though, the pilot must have forgotten. Or maybe, since it was a beautiful fall afternoon, he just decided to go for a drive in the country.

At any rate, the blimp drifted over the golf course, its sign trailing along behind. Herm and three other fellows were playing the ninth hole. (He gave us all this background information at the next board meeting.) Besides Herm, the group included the president of Dunlevy-Sanders Advertising Agency, the Chamber of Commerce executive director, and the treasurer of National Steel.

"Say," one of them said, "that's your blimp, isn't it, Herm?"

"Yes, it is. You're next, I believe."

"Looks beautiful up there. Wonderful idea. Every eye can see it. Outstanding example of institutional advertising."

"Yes," somebody agreed. (I think Herm said it was the head of Dunlevy-Sanders) "It's remarkable one other way, too. Almost any of the advertising media is limited to a particular class or income group. You choose the *Post*, and you reach the broad middle class. *Fortune* or the *Wall Street Journal* gets you a different group—quite selective. But that blimp up there—well, you can see that it gets through to us just as easily as it does to the day laborer."

"Ever think of broadening its appeal?" asks the Chamber of Commerce man.

"What do you mean?" Herm is interested.

Fortunately they were the only ones on the course that afternoon, and nobody was pushing to play through. So they just stood there at the ninth hole talking and looking up at the Gospel Blimp. You have to see it to realize how beautiful that blimp is against a brilliant blue sky when the leaves are turning. Of course the same thing is true at other seasons of the year, but I always thought it looked best in the fall.

"I mean that your blimp is sort of limited to a religious message. Now if you'd just broaden it a bit, the impact would be tremendous. Real piggyback advertising value."

"I get your point," says the Dunlevy-Sanders president. "Just like those institutional ads by Continental Can—those classic Great Ideas of Western Man ads."

"Right. Only in this case it would be a much closer relationship. I mean, what connection do tin cans or plastic bags have with Western civilization? But Christianity and Western civilization have grown up together. They're a natural. Pair them up and it does them both good. Piggyback."

"How would you do it?" Herm asks.

"Why, simply by carrying a second type of sign. Something like Free Enterprise Works. Or Support People's Capitalism. See what I mean? The potential would be tremendous. Tremendous."

"But," Herm objected, "what would that sort of an added emphasis do to the blimp's primary purpose? After all, the whole idea was a religious one. Now if we change that—"

"No need to change, Herm. Just add the other one on. As to what it will do to the religious impact, I have a hunch that it would increase it. Increase it. The new emphasis would bring a certain stability by tying your religious message into life today. That's my hunch, and my hunches have built up DS Advertising to a fifty million gross."

"I'm afraid it wouldn't work," Herm disagreed. "If for no other reason, we're dependent on a whole lot of religious people all over the country to support the Gospel Blimp. Costs close to eight thousand dollars a month. Monkey with the blimp's purpose, and that income could dry up overnight. It's hard enough getting money anyway today, without turning your supporters against you. No, I'm afraid the idea's out. Not that I don't think it's a good one, Mr. Sanders. I can see where the genius for your company's campaigns have come from. I'm not against the idea—it's brilliant."

"Ever think of new sources of income, Herm?" the National Steel treasurer asks.

"I dream about them every night!" Herm laughs.

"But few of my dreams materialize."

"Ever think of tapping the big corporations? Of getting money from some of the leaders in industry who aren't particularly religious?"

Herm shook his head. "They'd never get interested in the Gospel Blimp."

"Probably not. But they might get very much interested in this new idea. I'm pretty sure my company would. And we're just one of many. Think it over, Herm. That's my advice. Take it up with your board. If they're big men, they'll not miss an opportunity like this. Neither will you. It could mean a great deal to you personally."

"Thank you, sir. I'll certainly bring it up to my board."

And bring it up he did, at the next board meeting. It was on Friday night. Everybody was out, because Herm had passed the word around that something important was going to be presented. At Herm's request, the public relations fellow also was invited to sit in on the meeting.

Usually our board meetings were rather routine, mostly approving budgets and other business that Herm presented. For one thing, none of us had the time to put in on these things that Herm had, and so we just figured we had to have confidence in his recommendations.

Herm took devotions at the beginning of the meeting this particular night. He strung together a lot of different Bible passages, starting with the one about being wise as serpents and harmless as doves. Then he read a couple of parables: one about the men who were given the talents to invest, another about the tares growing among the wheat. He ended up with several verses about prayer being answered. Then he called on the public relations fellow to pray. (Usually we had a round of prayer, but not tonight.)

After we've disposed of a few other items of business, Herm says he has something new to present—something we may even be opposed to initially. But he wants us to listen with open heads before we come to any decision. And he'd like not to be interrupted with questions until he's given us the whole picture.

So he begins by giving a sort of summary of everything that's happened since that first summer night in George and Ethel's backyard (only he doesn't name them). He goes through all the developments, all the problems we've licked, all the things we've accomplished.

"If we're realistic," he says, "we've done a fair job of evangelizing our city. Maybe not perfect, but nothing human's perfect. At any rate, everybody's seen the Gospel Blimp. It's been a great testimony. Great.

"Now we've come to a possible major breakthrough. Up to this point we've been a rather small operation. Oh, I know it's seemed big—backbreaking at times. But is this our horizon? Have we reached the summit of Everest? Or is there more land to be possessed? I think there is. I think the past up to this moment is only introductory, that a step of faith at this point—well, I think you'll agree with me after I've told you what I have to propose."

So he tells us about what happened last week on the golf course, about Mr. Sander's suggestion. Then he ends by giving us his opinion, which is that we ought to go along with the idea.

"I know that some people, perhaps even some of you fellows on the board, will think this is a compromise, that we ought to continue to be just what we've always been. But you've got to be realistic. If we're going to advance, if we're going to forge ahead, why, I think there's only one way. At least it's the only way I've heard up to the present time. If any of your fellows have anything else to suggest, why, I'll be glad to listen. Floor's open for discussion. Or a motion."

Several of us jump in at the same time.

One says that he feels when God has raised up something like the Gospel Blimp, we ought to be awful careful about changing it.

Herm replies that there is no question about a change. There would be no change in the ministry of the blimp. Absolutely no change. This would only mean that a new emphasis would be added.

But, another asks, wouldn't it mean less hours for the gospel signs? How can you have both without the gospel being affected?

Maybe, Herm suggests, we could combine the two types of signs. He's just thinking off the top of his head, he says, but it does seem like a distinct possibility.

We went on like that for a couple of hours, nobody really satisfied with Herm's plans for the blimp. Nobody, that is, except the public relations fellow. He sided with Herm on every point.

Finally it came to a vote, or at least it would have come to that. But Herm saw which way the wind was blowing, so he suggested that instead of voting tonight, we appoint a committee to meet with Mr. Sanders and a few other men, business executives. Then the committee could report back and we'd be in a position to decide at our next meeting.

That sounded reasonable, so we tabled the matter and Herm appointed himself and two other board members, plus the public relations fellow, to the committee. Soon afterward we broke up for the night.

TEN
Those Worldly Griscoms

ON THE WAY HOME I passed by George Griscom's house. I hadn't seen him for weeks, and I didn't want him to think our friendship had been affected by his dropping off the blimp. So I decided to stop, even though it was getting a bit late.

Their place was sort of dark, only one light on downstairs. In a few minutes Ethel came to the door, her hair half up in curlers.

"Come on in," she says. "It's certainly been a long time since we've seen you. George will be so sorry he missed you."

"George away?" I ask. "I shouldn't really have stopped, it's so late. But you know how it is. I'm on my way home from the blimp board meeting, and I thought I'd just stop by to say hello."

"I'm certainly glad you did. We were talking about you and your family just the other day. George was saying we'd have to have you over for a lasagna supper or something. Yes, George is away until Sunday afternoon. He went to the shore with the man next door. You know, the one everybody's been praying for so long.

He's got a small boat and they'll be doing some fishing out in the bay. Maybe the ocean, too, not far out. But George hopes it'll just be the bay," she ends with a little laugh. "He gets deathly sick in any sort of rough water. He turns positively green. You should see him."

"No, I won't come in tonight. It's too late, and besides, I mainly wanted to see George. Thought I'd bring him up to date on the Gospel Blimp. This guy next door—has he become a Christian?"

"Not yet. But we're praying for him."

"So are we. And the Commander's not forgetting either."

"I know. The blimp comes over the neighborhood pretty often. And the bombs really clutter—I mean, there are a lot of them dropped. Just the other day George was mentioning it while he was cleaning out the downspout."

"Well, I'd better be getting home. Tomorrow I've got to do some painting and cleaning around the hangar. It's a full day's work, so I want to start early. So I'd better be getting home and to bed. Tell George I stopped, and tell him"—here I sort of laughed—"tell him I hope he's not falling into bad company since he got off the blimp board. What I mean is, we'd love to have him back. And you know how it is when you get away from Christian fellowship and with a beer-drinking, card-playing crowd. Not that I want to mind George's business, but you know how it is. But we'll be praying."

"Thanks. George'll be glad you stopped." She seemed to hesitate, then she said it real fast, so fast I almost missed it as I started down off the porch. "It's easy to get out of the world on a blimp, isn't it?"

Out of the world on a blimp? I though about it all the way home, but I couldn't quite figure out what she meant. Oh well. Ethel is probably just browned off about the blimp going so well and their not being involved in it any longer. I sure hope George hasn't started to drink or smoke. He's such a nice guy—it would be a shame to see him go down the river. But like they say, birds of a feather. I'll have to bring it up for prayer, I decide, at the blimp prayer meeting Sunday afternoon. And the women will have to remember Ethel, too. Her not seeming worried about George. That's something. Wonder if they ever were really one with us?

At any rate, I'm glad he's no longer on the board. It'd just take one guy who doesn't believe in the separated life to put the blimp on the skids. Really on the skids. But so far the Lord's been good to us. Taking George off, and keeping us from a split. Really good.

Eleven
Some Bright New Signs

A FEW WEEKS LATER the blimp started to carry the new type of signs. They were beautifully designed (DS Advertising had done them), and for the first few days, until we got fresh gospel signs, there was quite a contrast. The gospel ones had been out in all sorts of weather for over two years now. So they were sort of shabby and worn. You never realized it, though, until the new type were used.

Besides, there were a few changes that had to be made in the gospel signs when the new emphasis was added. For instance, as Mr. Sanders pointed out to the board, it was sort of funny coupling "All Have Sinned" and Free Enterprise the Perfect System together. They were, in his words, sort of incompatible. Same way with "I Am the Way" and "My Way's the American Way."

Since I was one of those on the board who questioned this new approach when Herm first brought it up, I suppose I ought to tell you that it really seemed to go over. For one thing, the fellows in the office where I work gradually seemed to change in their attitude toward the blimp. They now had sort of a respect for it, and you could have knocked me over with a feather when one day the boss called me into his office and gave me a check for IGBI.

Of course the guys outside in the plant weren't too favorable toward the blimp, especially after the new emphasis was added. They'd make cracks whenever I had to go out there from the office for something. Cracks like, "The blimp's wearing a white collar now," and "Blimps and bosses are full of hot air."

The women on the subassembly line also really began to rib me. One of them would scream, "Save me, save me," whenever I poked my head in the door.

"I will save you," someone across the room shouts back.

"Who are you to save me?" the first girl yells.

"I'm the president of National Steel," she answers. "Come unto me and rust." Then they all go into gales of laughter.

Ignorant people. Members of unions. It's that sort of people who don't appreciate the free enterprise system. Blasphemous, almost, the way they'll pervert Scripture to their own ends sometimes. Like I just quoted, "Come unto me and rust." But then, they don't know the Lord, so you can understand, sort of, their mixing Scripture up with their prejudices.

Financially God was pouring out His blessing upon the blimp. Some donors fell off, and we got a few letters disagreeing with the new emphasis. But in the main Christian people stood with us, especially after we told them of the way these other Christians were disagreeing with us on the change. That seemed to make the Lord's people rally round the blimp, I guess to make up for the break in the ranks.

But the big financial boost came from all these

important men and corporations and foundations. Only way I can explain it is a miracle, a miracle by which God worked in their hearts.

And we also got a whole lot of good advice and practical help as a result of the change. Herm saw to it that the board was enlarged so these big men could be included on it. One of the top lawyers in the city took care of changing the constitution, and he didn't even have to go to the state capital. When I think of all we went through to get that constitution and the charter in the first place, it really seems wonderful we could get the change made so easily.

Everything was sort of like that. Expert advice, the very best that was available, on every question. When the next year's budget was discussed, the treasurer of National Steel had all sorts of charts prepared to show projected donations, business trends, and other factors, on the basis of which we could determine our rate of expansion.

I guess our choice of verses to carry on the blimp must have been pretty hit-or-miss before the new emphasis. About all we did was pray about it. But when these new men got on the board, after its reorganization, especially Mr. Sanders, we sure weren't walking around in the dark any longer. His agency did marketing research on slogans and came up with answers in black and white. I tell you, he sure knew what he was doing. And he could make it all so plain to us through visual presentations.

Like I said, God really honored this new step of faith. It almost made you ashamed when you thought of how we floundered around in the early days of the blimp.

From then on the Gospel Blimp was really organized. You could feel it in every part of the work, from the spacious new offices with their modern furniture and illuminated map of the city, to the regular maintenance program on the blimp.

At long last we were in good with all, or almost all, the Protestant ministers in the city. Each Saturday we advertised a different church on the blimp. If any Sunday school had a contest, the winner was given a blimp ride. Most churches even had a special "Blimp Stewardship Sunday." We provided free church bulletins, with a photo of the blimp against a blue sky and a church steeple and an American flag on the front, and a low-key write-up about the blimp on the back. As a result, more and more churches put us in their budgets.

Same way with the city itself. Everyone was speaking well of us. This was partly due, I'm sure, to the caliber of new men who were on the IGBI board. But we were also doing little things to show our responsible community relations, things like running a sign "Don't Forget to Vote" on Election Day, taking part in parades, and other things like that.

Things had been going that way for several months, and it just made you thankful, also sort of proud, that you'd had a part in the original blimp vision. We often spoke of it at board meetings.

It hardly seemed possible that almost three years had passed since the idea first occurred to us. So one night I was surprised to get a phone call from George Griscom.

"Know what next Friday is?" George asks, after we've said hello, and how are you, and all the rest.

"Next Friday? No, can't say I do. Some sort of holiday?"

"No," he replies. "Something happened next Friday three years ago. Remember—you were over at our house for a picnic supper."

"Wait," I interrupt. "Now I know. That was the night we had our idea for the Gospel Blimp. A lot's happened since then."

"Sure has. Ethel and I were just talking, and we got to wondering if it wouldn't be a nice idea to invite everybody over next Friday who was here that night three years ago. Sort of a celebration, auld lang syne and all that."

"Sounds like a wonderful idea. I'm glad that you're still, well, I mean—"

"Still interested in IGBI and the blimp? Sure we are, though we haven't had much time to spend on it. And, of course, you know we haven't agreed with everything that's gone on. But Friday night we won't have to go into all that. We can just have a picnic supper, and remember the good old days."

"Well, count on us. I don't know about the rest, but we'll certainly be there. Anything we can bring—potato salad or ham or anything?"

"No, just your appetite," George says with a laugh. "Ethel will take care of everything."

I asked around and found that everyone had the same sort of phone call and invitation from George, only I didn't find out about Marge. And they all planned to be there except Herm. It seems he had a previous engagement.

TWELVE
Fulfillment

FRIDAY NIGHT CAME, a beautiful summer evening. We were the first ones there, and we found George in the yard, trying to hurry a charcoal fire along. "Welcome," he says. "You're just in time to help me get this fire going. Also to meet my friend and next-door neighbor."

This fellow I didn't know, but recognized, and was standing up by this time, having been kneeling next to the grill and blowing into it.

I was surprised, but I didn't say anything about it, even after I was alone with George. (The neighbor went into the house with my wife to help Ethel bring some things outside. I found out later that his wife was there, too.)

Seemed sort of funny to introduce somebody like this to the group. And I was sure that even if I was quiet about it, everybody else wouldn't be. Before the evening was over somebody was sure to say something to George and Ethel.

Especially since the neighbor was smoking. I hasten to add that smoke doesn't particularly bother me, but there are some that it does. And even though it wasn't so bad out in the yard as it would have been indoors, there were some who would certainly not appreciate the introduction of this worldly element to our Christian circle.

As different people came, you could tell they were surprised and a little put out to find the next-door neighbors there. And smoking. It just sort of took the edge off the celebration. Not that anyone said anything to the neighbors—we were all nice enough to them. It was more the little remarks people made to each other. George and Ethel couldn't help seeing our reaction.

I must say that Ethel pulled out all the stops on that supper. She had everything, ending with ice-cold watermelon, the first of the season.

George had just collected the rinds in a bucket, and we were all sitting around on deck chairs and folding chairs. Somebody tried to strike up "I'm So Happy, and Here's the Reason Why," but everybody was too full to be much interested in singing. So she gave up after a few lines.

At this point George sets the bucket down and begins to talk to the group. He recalls how we were all here three years ago, and how it was a night just like tonight. Even an airplane going over like it's going over just now.

We all look up at the twinkling lights.

"That night," George says, "we had the idea of a Gospel Blimp for the first time. And that's the reason we're celebrating tonight—what brings us together. But that's not all. If you remember, the thing that got us thinking about evangelizing the city that night was my next-door neighbors. They were sitting on the·porch, if you'll recall.

"And during the past three years there's been a lot of

prayer that these neighbors would become Christians, that they'd put their trust in Jesus Christ.

"Tonight I invited them over to have supper with the group because—well, to cut it short, God has answered our praying. They've become Christians."

Well, you should have heard the group when George told us that. We were really excited. Everybody wanted to ask questions at the same time.

"Was it a verse on the blimp or a fire bomb?"

"Day or night? I mean, was the verse in electric lights?"

"It must have been while we were still using the PA system. Do you remember what Herm said in his message?"

"Did you both accept the same invitation—I mean, at the same time the invitation was given over the PA system?"

"What tract was in the fire bomb? And did you fill in the decision cards?"

"Hey," George says, loud enough to be heard. "Hey, give them a break. One question at a time. And don't jump to any conclusions. Let them tell you."

So we finally quiet down, and the next-door neighbor begins to speak.

"Like George told you, we're Christians now. Both of us. But it wasn't the blimp."

"It wasn't?"

"You mean the blimp didn't save you, the Lord saved you? That what you mean?"

"No, I mean God didn't use the blimp. Fact of the matter is, the blimp irritated me, to put it mildly. Always cruising over our place and bothering us with that PA system, and dropping trash—that's what I considered it then—dropping trash on our lawn and in the rain gutters."

"But we were praying you'd be saved through the blimp."

"Sure, and God answered. But not by the blimp."

"But by people connected with the blimp."

"Well, not exactly. At least not while they were spending all of their time on the blimp. I mean George and Ethel. We've already told them, so I can tell you that we thought they were lousy neighbors."

"Lousy neighbors? But they were awfully concerned for your soul's salvation. You should have heard them pray for you at the regular prayer meetings."

"I did. It was once when the women met over here, and I was working out in my yard. I heard Ethel pray for us, that we'd be saved. But they were still lousy neighbors. Always busy working on blimp business, never any time for us. We'd invited them over for an evening, or have tickets for the ice hockey game. Once it was the garden show. But no matter what it was, they didn't have time for us. They only seemed to have time for the blimp."

"Remember that night we were going over accounts and he stopped by?" George asks, turning to me. "That night he invited Ethel and me to go to the shore. But I turned him down—blimp meetings Saturday and Sunday. That's the way we were."

"Sorry, George. I didn't mean to make it so strong," the next-door neighbor says. "It's just that—"

"No," George interrupts, "don't back down on what you said. That's the way we were. Stinking neighbors. Ethel and me. But we're glad you're not just neighbors now, but friends. And a brother and sister in Christ. That's what counts. Really counts. Well, folks, guess maybe we'd better think about breaking up. We don't want to keep you too long. We did promise some of you we'd break up early."

"Wait a minute, George," the neighbor says. "I haven't told the people how we became Christians."

"Sure you have." You can tell George wants it to end there.

"Let him go on, George," I say. "It's not too late, and besides, anybody with a baby-sitter who has to get home can leave. Let's hear the rest. We've got plenty of time."

"It won't take more than a few minutes to tell you the rest," the next-door neighbor says. "I don't want to keep you. But the last thing in the world I'd want you to leave thinking is that we're criticizing George and Ethel. Why, they've been Christ Himself to us ever since that second time the wife went into the hospital."

"Ethel came to see me every day," his wife explained. "I was so terribly discouraged that I had to go back in. But Ethel would visit me, and bring some flowers from her garden and just sit and talk. She was always so cheery and understanding. She'd read to me, and she'd talk about Jesus Christ. I'd never met anyone before to whom He was real. It seems strange, but I never had."

"I was awfully low, too," said her husband. "But George and Ethel had me over here for supper every night. And after supper George would read the Bible and pray at the table. He didn't read a lot, but what he read made sense. And I was struck with the same thing that struck the wife: Jesus was real to these people. They weren't putting on a show for our benefit.

"Like just before the wife came home from the hospital. Any of you guys ever spend two weeks keeping house with the wife away? You know what I mean—everything all crudded up. Not just egg stuck to the plates—egg stuck to the egg, which is stuck to the plates.

Bed linens, towels. You know how it is. Well, Ethel came in the day before and gave that house the going-over of its life."

"Yes," his wife added, "and for a month after I got home she wouldn't let me do a stitch of washing or ironing. Took all our dirty clothes home and did them."

"That's about it," the next-door neighbor finished. "We could tell you more—like George going to the shore Saturdays to fish with me, even when he knew I had beer in the cooler. Sure, I knew how you felt about drinking, George—but you weren't a Holy Joe about it. If you had been, I'd probably never had been interested in doing anything with you. And we'd probably not have become Christians."

There is silence. Everyone's thinking.

"Well," I finally say, "that was interesting. But I've got a big day tomorrow—I'm planting some perennials out at the entrance to the hangar. So I guess I'd better call it a night. Yes, it's been quite a night. Always wonderful to find out that God has answered prayer. He never fails, does He?"

"Sure doesn't," someone agrees. "Maybe not the answer we thought, but He always answers."

A sudden thought strikes me. "Hey," I say to the next-door neighbor, "how about coming out to the hangar with me tomorrow and working on the blimp? You'd enjoy it."

"Sorry," he says. "George and I are going bowling with the guy across the street."

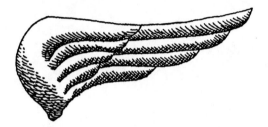

Gooley & Friends

THIRTEEN

I Saw Gooley Fly

HERB GOOLEY WAS JUST an ordinary sort of guy until the night he stepped out of his third-floor dorm window and fell away into the wild blue yonder.

But I'm getting ahead of my story.

I first met Gooley in that little hamburger and malt joint just off campus—Pete's Place. I'd never have noticed the guy except that he dropped a mustard bottle, and the stuff squirted down the front of his storm jacket. Now I'm a sophomore at the time, and this guy's a frosh. (No mistaking them during those early weeks of the quarter.) But he's making such a mess out of wiping the stuff off that I help him. Brother, what a mess. But Herb was the sort of fellow who could hardly wipe his nose himself, let alone the mustard.

When we had the stuff pretty well wiped off his coat and shirt (you could still see these bright yellow streaks), I ask him where he sacks out.

"Pollard," he says.

"That hole. Must be a frosh, huh? You'll learn. 'Course you can transfer after a quarter. Me, I'm at Sigma Phi House. Know the place that looks like a country club over on Lincoln?"

He doesn't know it. So we pay Pete and walk out. That is, I walk out. Herb trips over a cigarette machine that stands near the door.

Next time I notice the guy is at homecoming.

It's during the frosh-soph tug-of-war. (They really had pressure on those fire hoses that year.) We're ready for the final pull and the gun goes off. Suddenly the whole frosh team's yelling to stop pulling. So, after they turn the hoses on us, we stop; and here's Gooley, looking sort of dazed, with the rope twisted clear around his arm. I'll never know how he did it. They get it off and take him to the infirmary. Nothing broken, but he sure must have had a painful arm for a few days.

I remember—sometime the following fall—seeing a crowd gathered around the front of Hinton's department store. So I pull over to the curb, and here is the college station wagon half-in, half-out of Hinton's show window. What a scene. Bodies all over the place, one of them broken in two across the hood. Gooley's standing there holding a plastic head.

Maybe losing his driving privileges for a while got him interested in flying. At any rate, he comes back from Christmas vacation, his junior year, able to fly. Able to fly, mind you, not just able to fly a plane.

His roommate (Jerry Watson, it was) told us about it the next day. Seems Gooley had been studying late, and finally he turns the book over, switches off his desk light and says, "Think I'll go down to Pete's for a malted."

"Too late," Jerry says. "It's three minutes to twelve and he closes at midnight."

"I'll fly down." Gooley says it matter-of-factly, just like he's saying he'll run or something.

So over to the window he goes (Jerry all the while

thinking Gooley is suddenly developing a sense of humor), lifts it up, and steps off the ledge.

Their room is on the third floor.

Jerry waits a second for the thud, then dashes into the hall and down the stairs yelling, "Gooley fell out the window! Somebody call a doctor!"

No Gooley on the ground, or anywhere around. So they think Jerry's pulling their leg.

"Honest, fellows, Gooley stepped out of our window. Said he'd fly down to Pete's. Honest, he did."

So they wait around for Gooley to come back, and when he does, they start firing questions.

"Sure I can fly. Jerry was telling you the straight stuff. Here I'll show you." And with that he takes off into the wild blue yonder.

None of us believed the story when we heard it. Would you? In the first place, people can ride bicycles, people can row boars, people can fly planes even, but nobody can fly.

In the second place, if anybody could fly, Herb Gooley wasn't the man. That guy couldn't even walk.

It began to snow about suppertime the next day, and it snowed all through the night. Next morning the ground is covered, but some of the walks are shoveled off. I'm walking down the cleared path at the quad when I notice something. Fresh footprints go out on the snow a few yards, then there's nothing. Nothing. No trampled snow, no feet turning around. Just footprints going out and stopping.

Within a few days nobody needs any more circum-stantial evidence. We've all seen it—Gooley flying.

He'd be walking along with you, and suddenly he's airborne. Nothing spectacular. I mean it was all very quiet. His rise was almost vertical, and he flew along at about fifteen or twenty miles per hour. Just above the treetops. He'd sort of bank to turn.

That winter and spring you should have seen Gooley come into class on the third or fourth floor of Old Main. Brother, that was a sight to behold. It got to be a regular custom to open the window just before the bell. I'll never forget the day we had a visiting lecturer. Nobody had told him.

Let me tell you there was a run on the library for books on aerodynamics, aircraft design, and any other subject that even faintly bears on flying. Guys were spending all their free time soaking up all they could learn. So were most of the girls.

I don't want you to get the idea that we talked about it. Nobody would admit that he wanted to fly, but most everybody did. Nothing in the world I wanted more. (Seems sort of funny now.)

The college flying course tripled in size. (Flying planes, that is—but it was as close as we could come to personal flight.) In bull sessions we talked into the small hours about how Gooley probably did it.

You see, Gooley wasn't saying.

Of course, later there was some reaction—a lot of people began to call Gooley a freak. It sort of made us laugh, though, when one of the most outspoken anti-Gooleyites was found with a brain concussion at the foot of the Old Zach monument. (He got over it all right.)

I think the college administration was sort of ashamed to have Gooley as a student. So they bring in this guy Sevorsky for a special lecture series called "Flight Emphasis Week." Brother, were those lectures packed out. Standing room only.

Halfway through the week we realize that Sevorsky can't fly. We're standing outside Old Main, waiting for him to leave the president's office, which is on the second floor. So how does he come down? Why he walks down the stairs and out the front door. This guy can design airplanes, we say; he has the latest scoop on jets and helicopters; but he can't fly.

About a dozen students show up for his final lecture.

Most of us had heard a myth about some ancient Greek who could fly until he got too near the sun. So we think maybe there's a clue. Interest switches to books on ancient Greek mythology, and the library puts them on the reserve shelf.

You know, I've always been surprised that Gooley didn't tell us how to do it, or at least how he did it. He couldn't help knowing how interested we all were. But he kept his mouth shut. So none of us learned to fly.

It's a funny thing, but I still have a sense of loss at not learning Gooley's secret. And the other grads have confessed the same thing to me.

What happened to Gooley? I've often wondered about that. He transferred that fall to another college where, they say, all the students know how to fly.

Fourteen
Ceiling Zero

My roommate is a guy named Gooley. Herb Gooley.

He transferred to this crummy little school in the boondocks about six months ago. When he first arrived, we were all asking why he left a big, well-known college at the beginning of his senior year. Everybody's heard of it; nobody's heard of us.

Only thing we have that they don't have is a flight school. What they have, and we don't have, would fill a book.

One night I ask Herb straight out, "Why did you come here?"

"One reason," he says. "Last Christmas vacation I learned to fly. So I decided to switch to a flight school, a place where everyone could fly. That's why I'm here."

I should explain that I don't mean flying planes or gliders or balloons or anything. I mean we can fly, period.

We can step out of a window and be airborne. I remember my first flight—it was while I was still in high school—off a barn in the Blue Ridge Mountains. Some of the guys and girls here have been flying ever since they were little kids.

So the reason Herb Gooley gave for coming here made sense. Except for one thing, which he couldn't have known before he came. It's the sort of thing you don't learn from a catalog.

Gooley is a sensitive guy—withdrawn. Doesn't talk to many people. But there's some reason for being as he is: for one thing, he got off to a bad start.

I've never seen a happier freshman than Gooley, when he first showed up. I don't mean that he was actually a freshman—like I said, he was a transfer senior. But he had that same stupid innocence.

One of those hot afternoons in September—like so many days when school has just begun—I was stripped to the waist, arranging my clothes on hangers, when this new student comes through the window. He flew in—our room is on the third floor of Derwin Hall.

"I'm Herb Gooley," he says, "Boy, have I ever been looking forward to coming here."

"To this crummy school? Why?" I ask.

He looks sort of surprised. "Why, because it's a flight school. You can fly, can't you? The other guys in this dorm can fly, can't they? And the girls—just think of having a flying date. Wow!"

Should I tell him straight off, or should I let him find out for himself?

I guess I'm sort of chicken, because I decide not to say anything. Let someone else tell him.

"Yeah, this is a flight school, all right. We can all fly, including the profs—and the administration. You can have that bed over there by the door, Gooley. And that dresser, and either closet, except that I've got my things in this one. The public relations department can fly, too. They prepare the catalog."

He doesn't say anything, but begins to unpack. First

thing out of his suitcase is a copy of *Aerodynamic Theory.* It goes on his desk.

Around five-thirty I head for the dining hall. "Coming along?" I ask.

"Not yet," Gooley says. "Don't wait for me. I want to finish here first. I'll be along before it closes."

So I walk on over and go through the cafeteria line. I find my crowd and sit down to eat with them.

We're on dessert, when there's a little stir over by the door.

"What do we have here?" someone asks.

"An exhibitionist."

"A new student, you can tell that. Nobody else would fly on campus."

Sure enough—it's Herb Gooley, my new roommate. He comes through the door and touches down gently, by the stack of trays and the silver holder. He's got a smooth technique.

Everybody gets sort of quiet. I don't know about the others, but suddenly I'm thinking about some of my flights in high school days.

"You're too late," this battle-ax who runs the cafeteria says. "We close at six-thirty."

The clock on the wall says six-thirty. She's absolutely right, which is what she always is.

"Serves him right," a girl going back for seconds on iced tea says, loud enough for Herb to hear. "He's just a show-off."

Gooley looks sort of hurt, but he doesn't say anything, either to battle-ax or to battle-ax, junior grade. He just heads out the door. Walking.

"He'll learn," someone at my table says. "We all learned."

And he did, during the next few weeks.

First thing he finds out is that here nobody flies. In spite of this being a flight school, and everyone can fly—theoretically—we're all grounded.

There's a lot of talk about flight, of course, a daily flight hour. But nobody flies.

Some of us came here planning to be flight instructors. I myself wanted to teach Africans how to fly, but that didn't last long.

Actually, the deadest things are the flight courses. They use *Aerodynamic Theory* as the text, but you'd never recognize it. One flight out of a hayloft has more excitement to it than a year of that course.

One night we get into a discussion on our floor of the dorm.

"Look, Gooley," one of the guys says, "tell us about the college you were in before you came here. It is true that they have more exciting courses than we do here?"

"A lot of them, yes," Gooley says. "But they don't know anything about how to fly."

"Are the girls there real swingers?"

"I guess so. But they can't fly."

The way Herb answers sort of frustrates the guys who are asking the questions, because they would jump at a chance to transfer to the school he came from.

"I think this flying isn't all it's cracked up to be," one of them says.

"I feel the same way," another chimes in. "And besides, it seems sort of selfish to me to fly when the rest of the world is walking."

"Not only selfish. To them you look like some kind of a nut, up there above the ground. From here on in, any flights I take are going to be when there's nobody around to see me."

"Besides, the world needs to be taught how to walk.

And pavements and roads need to be improved."

"Did any of you read John Robin's book? It's a pretty strong critique of *Aerodynamic Theory*, and he does an effective job of questioning the usual foundations of flight. The significant thing is that Robin is a flyer, not a walker."

That was the only time I ever heard Herb Gooley swear. "Oh, hell," he says and dives out the window. (It was a cold night, but fortunately we had opened the window because the room was getting stuffy. If we hadn't, I think Herb would have gone right through the glass.)

He didn't return until early next morning. I heard him at the window and got up to open it. It had begun to snow, and he was covered. He looked nearly exhausted, but happier than I'd seen him since the day he first arrived.

That night marked a change in Herb Gooley, a change that came to affect the whole school. Only, I didn't know it at the time.

He began to fly again. On campus.

Now when you're with flyers, flying isn't remarkable—actually it's the basic minimum, it's taken for granted. What worries us is perfection, and it's sort of embarrassing—around other flyers—to try an extra little maneuver, or to stay aloft longer than usual. There can be such a letdown. And the competition is so keen. There's always someone who can fly better than you.

That's the reason nobody flies here. At least they didn't, not until Gooley took it up again.

Like the flight prof says, "This is a school for flying, not an airport. You've come here to learn more about flying, not to fly. We want to teach you how to fly with real conviction." Then he draws diagrams on the blackboard. And he walks across the campus.

Meanwhile, Herb is getting better and better. I mean his flying is improving. You can see him on a moonlit night, trying all sorts of flight gymnastics.

Moonlit nights. That brings me to another side of the change in Gooley.

He began to have flying dates. Not many—none of the girls, except one or two, would be caught dead on a flight date, especially with Herb.

What can you talk about on a flying date? What can you do? I ask you.

We discuss it while Gooley's out of the dorm. He's out a lot those last months of school. Not just flying or on flight dates, but teaching a bunch of kids to fly at the community center in town, studying *Aerodynamic Theory* with a little group of students. The guys can't understand why Herb keeps at it.

"Sure we can fly—at least as well as that guy Gooley. But after all, real life is down here on the earth. It's not as if we were birds.

"Besides, we've got to learn to relate to the walkers. And that's a lot harder to do than flying."

"I've found—I don't know about the rest of you guys—but I've found that they're not much interested in my flying ability. I mean, the walkers aren't. So it's important to show them that I can walk."

"Don't get me wrong. It's not that I'm against flying. I'm not. But you don't have to fly to be for flying."

So the year ends.

We graduate.

I ask Gooley, while we're packing, what he plans to do next year.

"Grad school," he says. "In a walking university. You see, I was reading *Aerodynamic Theory* the other day, where it says that you can take off best against the wind.

FIFTEEN
Mayday

I PASS THE MAIN GATE, not intending to enter. Then I see the sign—MAY DAY CELEBRATION—stretched between two old elms.

Mayday, international distress call, ship going down, airplane in grave peril.

Mayday, Communism's fearful growth, Russia in shambles to half the globe in half a century.

I turn in through the gate.

The sun, lowering on the horizon, highlights a tree-lined walk. In the distance, old stone buildings are outlined against the sky. Lawns, well-kept, flow down from the building.

"Welcome to our May Day celebration, sir. May I help you find someone?"

Young, courteous, graceful. Her hair in soft curls, not straight and unbecoming. Her skirt a proper length.

"Are you looking for someone in particular? Or have you come to help us celebrate May Day?" She spoke again.

"I know no one here. I only came to see the grounds, perhaps to visit the library and chapel. I suppose it was the May Day sign that led me to enter."

"Our celebration begins soon. But first, I'll take you to our library. We're quite proud of it."

Up the concrete path to the nearest building. Young men and women stroll beneath the trees.

Not even hand in hand. A proper distance between. And chaperoned. Not like so many young people today.

"Here we are, sir. Don't we have a nice library?"

Small, but carefully kept. Not many at the tables, reading—probably the celebration has taken the attention of most.

Over to the card file.

Marbel. Markham. Marlborough. Marx, Groucho. Marx, Groucho. Marx, Groucho. Marx, Groucho. Mary, Mary.

The little woman at the checkout desk looks up.

"Are the cards on Karl Marx being retyped or collated?"

"No, we have no books on Karl Marx." She smiled pleasantly.

"Communism, then?"

"None on Communism either."

"Where's the chapel building, please?"

"I'll take you." It was the young lady again. "Vespers have begun. It will be filled because it's a special day."

Into the Gothic building, a stone in a green setting.

"God is love; love is God. God loves us; we love God. He understands us; we understand Him. He cares for us; we care for Him."

See God run. Run, God, run. Run. Run. Run.

"Peaceful peace from the God of love. And now a closing hymn."

Follow the gleam, gleamel the foll, low the gleamoofel, gloff the fleamow.

"Everyone is so quiet and reverent."

"Thank you, sir. We're quite proud of our chapel."

"Tell me, does he ever deal with problems?"

"Problems? What sort of problems, sir?"

"War, for instance."

"But he did, sir. Just now. you hear him mention peace, didn't you? He's always positive. Isn't that the best way? But perhaps there's some other problem you had in mind?"

"Race?"

"Oh, sir, you're funny. Of course we'll have a race. That's part of the celebration—the May Day celebration each year. But there's no problem about race!"

"No problem, indeed. A race is a lot of fun. Now what do we do?"

"We hurry over to the maypole. There, do you hear the music? They've started already. Let's run. This is the big event of our May Day celebration. We all—that is the girls—get a chance to dance around the pole. See, there it is—over there, behind the dining hall. Isn't it beautiful?"

"Beautiful it is. And the music—it's lovely and quiet."

"That's our string quartet, sir."

"Do you have a rock group? Or folk music?"

"No, they're not permitted. But actually, even though some of us liked rock and folk music at home, we really prefer strings here. Sometimes we have a brass ensemble too. It stirs you."

"Aren't you going to join the dance around the maypole?"

"I'd like to. Will you excuse me for a few minutes, sir?"

"Of course. But come back."

Mayday. Mayday.

May Day. May Day.

Maypole, maypole. Over and under and up and through, near and beyond, far and down, past and by, forth and over and around and back.

"Back so soon?"

"Yes, I got tired. And besides, if we're not going to have to wait a long time, we'd better go over to the dining hall and get in line. You will eat with us, won't you?"

"If they're set up for guests. I really wasn't planning to stay for supper when I came, though."

"Tonight, guests are welcome. It's all part of the May Day celebration."

"It's a pretty big dining hall."

"Yes, a thousand people can eat here at one time. But what takes time is going through the cafeteria line. Not that I'm complaining. They are really doing the very best they can."

The dining hall isn't open yet, but the line is already a block long. Yet it is quiet—orderly. No pushing or rowdyism.

"Everybody is so polite. And quiet."

"Of course. They discourage loud talking. And we want to do what they want us to do."

"After supper, what's on the program?"

"Something very special, sir. We have a drama group— I'm in it—and tonight we're putting on a play."

"Modern? Ibsen? Shaw? Miller?"

"No. Who are they, sir? Our plays are written by our very own Mr. Jackson. We also do Gilbert and Sullivan sometimes. But I can't sing, so I'm not in them."

"Do you ever have any protest meetings?"

"Protest? Against what?"

"This long line, for instance. Or the quality of the

food. Or bigger things—national policy, things like that."

"Oh, no, sir. We would never think of protesting anything. We know they wouldn't like it. There, now, it didn't take us long to get inside the dining hall, did it? You can pay for your meal down there at the far end of the line, down past the steam table. Sometimes I work on the steam table. I sort of like doing that."

"Are you working your way through?"

"Working my way. . . . Oh, there's someone I want you to meet. My counselor. Here he is. I don't know your name, sir."

"How do you do. I'm Muriel's counselor."

"And I'm just an out-of-town stranger, passing by. I saw the May Day celebration sign and decided to come in. And I'm glad I did. I'm really impressed. I have a daughter who is just eighteen—do you think she would be accepted here?"

"Is she somewhere else? I mean, would it involve a transfer?"

"No, she would be entering here for the first time."

"Well, the place to begin is to see your family doctor about commitment."

SIXTEEN
Rehoboam's Gold Shields

REHOBOAM CHECKED IN today, about four o'clock this afternoon. He walked into the dorm, looked around the way every freshman does, and headed for the room he'd been assigned to. Then he went back out to the car and brought in his gear.

Nothing unusual about Rehoboam's arrival—except that among his things were some gold shields. And those shields are the cause of no little comment around the dorm. He can tell.

A shield is an awkward thing, difficult to wrap, impossible to stow away so it doesn't show. Maybe Rehoboam wouldn't have been so conspicuous, if anybody else had brought shields. But nobody had.

"Why does a guy bring shields to a university?" he hears as he enters the john. But that's the end of the conversation, at least until he leaves.

Those first few days everyone finds some excuse to come to Rehoboam's room. "What's the text for Chem 101?"

"When's the deadline for dropping a course?"

"Do you know how much an extra season ticket costs?"

Sometimes they don't even wait for the answer before they wander over to the dresser, where the gold shields are stacked. (The things are too wide to fit in a closet.)

"Hey, look at the shields," they say. "First ones I've seen here at the university."

Always there's the same feeble, half-apologetic explanation by Rehoboam. They were his dad's shields, but his dad gave them to him. Then he warms to his subject a bit and explains that they're gold—believe it or not. Sure, they're worth a lot.

So they begin to call him the "Gold Shield Boy." Word gets out about the shields. Pretty soon it's all over the campus—even the profs know. Worst of all, the girls think it's a big joke.

Hardly a day passes that one or two guys don't come over to Rehoboam's dorm to see the shields. Several upperclassmen advise him to hang on to them—"They're worth more than most of the garbage you'll pick up around here"—but the general opinion seems to be that shields are out of place in a university, and a man must be some kind of nut to own them. Especially gold ones.

After four or five weeks of this, day after day, night after night, a certain change begins to take place in Rehoboam. Defending his shields is wearing him down. He spends as little time as possible at the dorm, hangs around the union a lot, and studies at the library. A conviction grows in his mind that he's a fool to have brought those gold shields along to the university.

One morning, as he dresses hurriedly so he can grab breakfast before an eight o'clock class, he notices something. One shield is missing. Sure enough—it's gone. No time to look for it now, though. Later on, after class, he'll come back and find it. But later in the day, when he gets time to hunt for the missing shield, he can't locate it. And it doesn't turn up later in the week.

Before long, a second shield disappears, then another. Rehoboam is determined to keep the last one from being stolen, for he values that one especially. But when he returns to his room one morning at four a.m., after spending a night in town, he finds that the last shield is gone too.

Surprisingly, his feeling, in the face of this great loss, is one of relief. Those gold shields won't make him stand out anymore. Now he's the same as everyone else. At last he can feel thoroughly at home in the university.

And he does. The gold shields gone, his defense of them ended, Rehoboam becomes a popular figure on campus.

As Christmas vacation approaches, however, some misgivings trouble him. What to do about the shields when he goes home?

The solution, when he finally thinks it through, is simple. He decides to replace the gold shields with others made of highly burnished brass.

He takes the counterfeit shields home with him when vacation begins, and his deception appears to be complete. None of his family seems to notice the substitution. The reaction pleases Rehoboam, for it would upset his family to learn of his loss, which he knows is a great one.

SEVENTEEN
Protest until Pizza

"SO WHAT ARE you going to do?"

"Do? What can I do—what can anyone do? It's done now, over, finished, *kaput.*"

"No marches?"

"Are you kidding?"

"No placards? No demonstrations?"

"Look, about that seventeenth-century lit assignment. . . ."

"You're a great one. March for better food in the dining hall, march for Professor Fliedner, march for graffiti on the library walls. Now suddenly, halt, one-two."

"Come off it. Let up, will you? Those things were free speech. This would be free suicide. Anything now would be putting our heads in a noose. Besides, I didn't see you at any demonstrations, even the big sit-in for Fliedner. You never carried a placard for free speech. So don't start trying to make me feel guilty. By the way, what do you intend to do now?"

"Nothing. I'm not going to change my pattern, which means I'm consistent."

"So am I. It's just that a new element, a radically different element, has entered the picture."

"Meaning Irving was dragged out of the dormitory?"

"Right. That and the Supreme Court decision last Friday. Now there's no longer any doubt about it."

"But what happens to free speech, if that's so?"

"It's still there. Nothing's happened to it."

"Provided you use it harmlessly—like trying to get visiting privileges in the girls' dorms extended to all night or something else that's strictly university."

"Sure, like that."

"But not Irving, picked up by the federal police last night. Not the prison camp outside of Peoria. Not the genetic test of fallout."

"Cool it. After all, I can't do anything about those things."

"You mean they're not like getting more steak in the dining hall, or pressuring the university to renew Fliedner's contract after they discover he's a Communist?"

"Right. There's some hope for results on protests like that. But Irving, prison camps—no hope. Absolutely none."

"What if Irving's headed for the extermination chamber?"

"All the more. Who knows—say I did protest—that the federal police wouldn't be knocking on my door tomorrow night. Then my days of usefulness would be over."

"Just like Irving's."

"Sure, like Irving's. Only he had no choice. I do."

Thank God you're not Jewish."

"Right. And you can, too."

"I do. Never more than today. But I got sidetracked. We were talking about demonstrations and free speech."

"You were talking. I'm finished."

"Don't you feel any responsibility to demonstrate against the government's policy toward Jews?"

"What good would it do?"

"I don't know. I guess it wouldn't change things."

"Right. The Supreme Court's decision makes it final."

"So Irving is thrown to the dogs."

"He has lots of company, if you've been reading the papers."

"But I know Irving personally. He's someone I've gotten my physics assignments from. I've talked about the World Series with him. I've eaten pizza late at night with Irving."

"But he's Jewish, and there's nothing you can do about it."

"I'd like to make a sign, Free Irving Greenhow, or The United States Is Murdering Jews, or maybe even, Get Haman out of the White House."

"What would you do with the sign?"

"Why, I'd carry it downtown—maybe to the newspaper office. Then I'd march with it."

"For two minutes maybe. After that you'd be on your way to Peoria. With only your teeth smashed in, if you were lucky."

"But what a glorious two minutes! It would almost be worth it."

"Nothing's worthy dying for."

"But Irving's not a thing. He's the person endowed with certain inalienable rights."

"Not any longer, he isn't. He's a nonperson without any rights at all. Maybe he's dead already."

"So steak is more important to you than Irving."

"I guess so. Or—give me the benefit of the doubt—

Fliedner's right to teach although he was a Communist? Some of the protests were more significant than others."

"You'd demonstrate for Fliedner's right to speak, but not for Irving's right to live?"

"I wouldn't put it quite that way, but I guess that's about it. The point is, we had a chance of gaining what we were after in Fliedner's case; none at all in Irving's. So why demonstrate?"

"Maybe to let them know we don't agree with what they're doing to the Jews. Or to say—here's Irving Greenhow—he's got as much right to live as anyone else. As me. Even as the President."

"But he doesn't. The Supreme Court answered that question last week. The Bill of Rights is relative; it's conditional."

"Isn't there any higher appeal than the Supreme Court?"

"Not in this country, there isn't. The Supreme Court is the end of the line."

"I know that. But beyond the court, even beyond the country. Isn't there any higher authority?"

"The UN stopped meeting two years ago. What's left?"

"What about you and me?"

"What about us?"

"Don't we have any responsibility to a higher authority?"

"Who? If you mean Irving—if you mean human dignity or something like that—it's too late. He's probably dead. Or soon will be."

"I mean God."

"God? What's He got to do with this? God's in church on Sunday mornings, not in demonstrations. God isn't carrying any placards. Not even for Irving."

"Maybe I owe it to God."

"Owe it to God? If you did, the preachers would be telling you, don't forget that. They're not."

"Maybe they value their lives as much as we do ours."

"Of course they do. If they got killed, or even put in prison, who'd keep church?"

"So everybody is silent because they—I mean we—might get killed if they spoke."

"Not might. Would. There's no doubt about it."

"That means life is more important than anything else in the world."

"Right. You'd better believe it."

"It also seems to say that life is more important than God."

"And it is, except for some misguided people in history who had a martyr complex."

"Including Jesus?"

"I don't really know. He's a hard one to figure out."

"And He didn't keep silent."

"And died for it."

"You know what? We've been talking so much we missed supper."

"Let's go downtown and get a pizza."

Meek Souls
& Phonies

EIGHTEEN
How Silently,
How Silently

HE ARRIVED AT Chicago's O'Hare airport on TWA Flight 801 from Israel. The plane was two hours late, but the delay made little difference, since there was no one to meet him.

It was December 23, a Friday afternoon. The terminal building pulsed with people coming home for Christmas, relatives meeting people coming home, businessmen and students trying to get on flights for Cleveland and New York, Seattle and Atlanta, so they could be home for the holidays.

The Israeli had gone through immigration and customs in New York. He had no baggage, only a small airline bag with a broken zipper.

Christmas carols issued from concealed speakers the length of a long corridor into the main building, interrupted only by announcements of arriving flights, departing flights, boarding areas now open, passengers being paged. He walked down the corridor listening, watching people.

In the main terminal building a massive, white-flocked Christmas tree, decorated with golden balls stood in a corner beyond the telephone booths and rows of seats. He turned aside to examine the tree, then stepped onto an escalator marked Down to Baggage and Ground Transportation.

"Excuse me," he said to a pretty girl at the Avis counter, "can you tell me how to get to Wheaton, Illinois?"

"Easiest way is to rent an Avis car and drive there," she replied. "Only thing, we don't have any available. I'm sorry. Unless you have a reservation, that is. If you don't, you might try Number One over there."

"Thank you, but I don't drive. Is there a bus?"

"I don't think so. You'll have to take a cab."

He repeated his question to a man in uniform who stood near the door of the terminal, explaining that he didn't think he had enough money for a cab.

"Take this bus to the Loop," the man said. "Get off at the Palmer House, walk back to State Street, down State to Madison—get that? On Madison get a bus to the Chicago and Northwestern Station. You can get a train there for Wheaton. Bus is loading now."

The young Israeli murmured his thanks and walked outside the terminal building. He shivered as the sharp wind whipped through his light topcoat. It was snowing.

"Please tell me when we get to the Palmer House," he asked the bus driver.

"First stop," the driver said.

The bus cruised down the expressway. Lights and signs and thousands of cars. Trucks and shopping centers and Christmas trees and lights. Signboards in green and red, "Merry Christmas" in letters two feet high.

"Palmer House," the driver called.

The Israeli left the warm bus. A blast of cold air off the lake hit him as he stepped down to the sidewalk. His teeth chattered; he turned the ineffectual collar of his coat up around his neck.

At the corner he hesitated, then stopped to look at the jewels and expensive ornaments in Peacock's window. Then he hurried on, after asking a policeman which direction Madison Street was.

Almost running because of the cold wind and driving snow, he covered the three blocks to the other bus quickly. It was crowded; he stood between an elderly woman who kept sneezing into the elbow of her ragged coat, and a teenage boy, his arms full of packages.

At the Chicago and Northwestern Station he bought a ticket to Wheaton, then sat in the waiting room for half an hour. Once he went over to the newsstand to buy a paper. The front page had stories about war, politics and crime; a photograph of a wan child with leukemia, slumped in a wheelchair beside a smiling actress and a Christmas tree at Children's Hospital; a reminder of "One Shopping Day Left Before Christmas."

Finally he boarded the train. It was so hot inside, and he was so tired from his trip, which had started the previous day in the Middle East, that he fell asleep.

About an hour later the conductor shook him awake. "You want to get off at Wheaton, this is it."

The young Israeli stepped down onto the snow-covered station platform. He almost fell as his foot slipped on the smooth surface.

"Careful there, young fellow." The conductor clutched his arm.

He crossed the tracks to the sidewalk. As he looked uncertainly in both directions, a young woman smiled at him. She was was learning against a green Vega.

"Hi," she called.

"Hello," he answered. "So this is Wheaton."

"It is, for better or for worse."

"Is there any worse?"

"Yes. Me, for instance. You look cold. Where are you going?"

"I'm not sure."

"It's darned cold talking out here. How about coming up to my apartment? It's only a few blocks over—I'll drive you."

"Thank you. Do you live with your mother or someone?"

"No, I live alone. Say, are you from around here? Or maybe Glen Ellyn? I saw you get off the train."

"I'm from Israel."

"You're Jewish, aren't you?"

"Yes, I'm Jewish. And you're Mary."

"How did you know? Did someone tell you about me?" An edge of belligerence showed in her voice.

"You had to be Mary."

"What do you mean, I had to be Mary? Why couldn't I be Judy or Jean or Connie?"

"Because you're Mary."

"If you're from Israel, you're a long way from home. Do you have any friends here? I mean, is anyone expecting you?"

"Nobody's expecting me. And I haven't a place to stay, so I'm in the market for one."

"You can stay with me for a few days."

"Thank you, Mary. Any other suggestions?"

"I mean it. It'll be nice having company over Christmas. You won't put me out."

"Mary, I do appreciate your invitation, I do. But are there any other possibilities?"

"Well, there's a house over near my apartment building, where the lady takes roomers. She's really old—and safe. Maybe she'd have a room for you."

"Would you drive me there so I can find out?"

"Sure. Get in the car—you must be freezing."

"I am. This coat was made for Jerusalem, not Chicago."

"Or Wheaton. This is a cold place too."

The elderly lady had a room, which the Israeli took. He had barely enough money for one week's rent.

Mary saw him count out the bills, and saw how little was left in his wallet.

"Look," she said, "I just got paid. Let me give you something to tide you over."

"Mary, you're generous. I don't think I'll need it, though. After all, I'll only be here over Christmas."

"Well, as long as you don't forget that I'm ready to help you—no strings attached."

"No strings attached."

"Hey, it's almost seven o'clock and I haven't eaten yet."

"We had a big meal on the plane from New York, so I'm not hungry."

"Good. In that case I know where we can get enough to eat without having to pay for it. This Christian publishing company is having a sort of Christmas open house this evening. The public's invited to see their new building. We can go and fill up on cookies and punch."

"Sounds interesting. Let's go."

Mary drove several miles, then parked her car in the parking lot of a rather imposing one-story building.

"Look here," she said as they closed the car doors, "we don't have to stay very long."

"All right, Mary. By the way, what are those other buildings?"

"That one's Christian Youth headquarters, the next

one's Sunday School, the one down the road there is Congo Missions. Let's go in out of the cold."

Inside the building, a table was placed in front of a Christmas tree. The tree was decorated with hundreds of little Bibles, about the size of a child's hand, hanging from the branches.

The table was covered with a white cloth and decorated with holly. A poinsettia plant in the center was surrounded by sandwiches, Christmas cookies, a silver coffee service, plates, cups, napkins, and spoons. An empty punch bowl stood at one end of the table.

"I'm sorry we've run out of punch," said the lady seated at the other end of the table, "May I pour you some coffee?"

"Yes, please." Mary extended her hand for the cup.

"Could you get me some water, please?" asked the young Israeli. "Maybe just fill up the punch bowl."

"Oh, we won't need to do that," the lady replied. "That many people won't be wanting water tonight."

"Why don't you do like he says?" Mary asked. "Maybe he's really thirsty. Or maybe some other people will be. It's hot in here, you know. Or hadn't you noticed?"

"Certainly," the lady said. "Bob, could you come here a moment? Will you please fill the punch bowl up with water?"

Bob returned after several minutes, carrying the large bowl awkwardly because of its weight.

"Strangest thing happened," he said in an excited voice. "When I took it out in the kitchen it was empty, except for some ice. But when I turned the faucet on, and began filling the bowl, it wasn't like water at all. Look, it's dark red."

"Let's have a taste."

"I can't believe it, I really can't. There's—yes, I'm

sure it's wine in that punch bowl. Bob, tell us the truth. What really happened?"

"Just like I said. When the water from the kitchen faucet ran into the punch bowl, it turned to what's in there now. Honest it did."

"I haven't tasted that stuff in fifteen years, not since I was saved. But there's no doubt about it—that's wine, and it's the best."

"Bob, will you please take it back out in the kitchen and pour it down the drain? We can't have word get around that we served an alcoholic beverage here at our open house.

"I'm sorry about what's happened, sir," she said to the Israeli. "Would you like some coffee?"

"No, thank you. I'll just have some of these sandwiches and cookies."

A few minutes later, Mary suggested they leave. And they did.

"That was great," she said as they drove away in her car. "I don't know how you did it, but it was just great."

"I'm tired—I guess it must be the time change from Israel to here. You won't mind driving me back to my room now?"

"Of course not. And I won't even try to get you to stop at my apartment first."

Next morning the young Israeli slept late. When he left the house, he saw Mary waiting in her car at the corner. It had snowed all night, and the heavy flakes were still coming down.

"How long have you been waiting here?" he asked as he opened the car door.

"Oh, ten—maybe fifteen minutes. That's all."

"It would have taken a lot longer than that for the windshield to get this covered with snow." As he sat down in the warm car, he brushed the snow from his thin topcoat.

"Hey, I have something for you," she said.

"What is it, Mary? Say, will you please turn that radio down? I can hardly hear you, and I feel as if I have to shout to make myself heard."

"Sure. That's WLS, by the way. Here's what I got for you."

"A heavy coat and earmuffs! Mary, Mary. You knew how cold I was, and you bought me some warm clothes. Do you mind if I put them on right now?"

"I'll mind if you don't."

As they sat at breakfast in a small restaurant, Mary and the Israeli were silent for a long time. Finally the Israeli spoke.

"Mary, you're sick of it, aren't you?"

"Up to here." She put her hand to her mouth.

"Things will be different."

"They already are. I know you now. Please stay for a while."

"Not for long."

"Long enough to make sure the change is permanent?"

"It will be. I don't need to stay around here for that, Mary."

"Long enough to change this town?"

"No, I can't stay that long. Just until tomorrow night."

"Christmas night."

"Christmas night. Then I must leave."

"It's funny, having you here in Wheaton for Christmas. And funnier that I'm the only one who knows you're here."

"You were there at the Northwestern Station to meet me."

"Am I glad I was!"

"Let's finish our coffee and leave."

"Look, I have to work this afternoon. You take my car. You can drop me off, and maybe pick me up around six o'clock. Or I can walk home. It's not far. But you can use my car to get around in today."

"I don't drive. Thanks anyway, Mary. But I'll manage without transportation today. Especially with this warm coat." He smiled at her.

"Do you like it? I hoped you would. Now I'll have to get to work. How about meeting me for supper tonight? I'll stop by your house for you at six-thirty or seven. Then later we can go to the Christmas Eve service at church. I haven't been there for a while, but I'd like to go again.

"Fine, Mary. I'll be looking for you around six-thirty."

He walked all over town that afternoon, stopping at the county jail, a convalescent home, and the church parsonage.

A middle-aged, worried-looking woman answered the door at the parsonage.

"Yes?" she said.

"I am a stranger here, from Israel. I thought I'd stop by to meet the pastor."

"He's very busy today—the day before Christmas, you know, and Christmas on a Sunday this year. But step inside, I'll call him."

He waited inside the door for several minutes. Then the pastor came downstairs with his wife.

"James, this is a man from Israel who wants to meet you. I told him how busy you are this afternoon."

"Never too busy to meet one of the Lord's people. Welcome!" He gripped the younger man's hand. "Are you here for long?"

"Just through Christmas. I'll leave tomorrow night."

"Well, it's great to meet you. Will you be in church tomorrow? We're especially interested in Israel—our church supports two missionaries there. Israel General Mission. Know it?"

"I've heard of it."

" 'To the Jew first,' I always say. Maybe you'd share something with us at our morning service tomorrow. Our missionary conference is coming up in February and it won't hurt a bit to have a word about Israel and missions on Christmas Sunday morning."

"I'll be glad to speak."

"Just briefly, you understand. Five minutes at the most. We'll really be pushed for time tomorrow—special music, you know. Probably you have the same problem with time back home in Israel."

"Perhaps things are a little more simple there. Yes, I'll stick to the five minutes."

"Good. The Lord bless you. Is it still snowing out? I'll see you tomorrow—don't trip on the raised sill."

The Israeli returned to his room in the house where he was staying.

A little after six-thirty he saw the green Vega parked in front of the house. He heard a light sound of the horn as he went downstairs, pulling on his new, warm coat.

Mary leaned over to open the door. "It's great to see you again. I thought the afternoon would never end."

"I guess my afternoon went quickly because I did so much walking and saw so many different people. But I'm certainly glad to see you again, Mary."

"Look, is it all right with you if we go up to my apartment to eat?" Before he could answer, she added, "There will be other people there, friends of mine."

"I'd like nothing better."

"But we'll probably get talking and won't get to the Christmas Eve service at church. In fact, these friends of mine wouldn't go anyway. They're not the church kind. They're like me—like I was before I met you."

"Supper with you and your friends sounds a lot more interesting—and worthwhile—than sitting through a Christmas Eve service."

"Do you really mean it? I was afraid you'd be like the rest—oh, that wasn't a kind thing to say. I've got so much to learn."

By now they were climbing the stairs to the second-floor apartment. From inside the door came sounds of the Living Dead.

"It'll be noisy," Mary said as she opened the door. "Hi," she called out to the six or seven forms sprawled on chairs and on the floor. "Turn that record player down, someone. I want you all to meet my new friend. I've only known him one day, but in my whole life nobody has ever known me so well. He's from Israel."

"Welcome, Israeli. How are the Arabs?"

"Suffering, as they have for centuries. Like my own people."

"We'll eat soon, gang," Mary called as she went into the tiny kitchen. She turned toward the Israeli, "Come and help me."

Before long, spaghetti was overflowing a large bowl, and long loaves of bread, buttered and flavored with garlic, were placed on the table next to a bowl of green salad. The table had no cloth on it. paper plates and red paper napkins were set out, with stainless steel utensils.

When the food was on the table Mary announced, "Before we eat, my Israeli friend will pray."

There was a whisper, "Mary has a new hang-up."

The Israeli stood in the kitchen doorway. "Father,"

he said, "I thank You for this spaghetti and for Mary's kindness to us all. Make Your name glorious in this room tonight."

No one sat at the table. They ate from their laps, or placed their plates on the floor, where they sat or reclined. At first the music was so loud it was hard to talk, except to one other person. But as they were finishing the meal, Mary turned down the volume. Then the whole group began to discuss war and peace, sex and drugs, life, race (two of them were black), Camus and Christmas.

The Israeli listened most of the time, although he asked a lot of questions. His occasional comments were brief. He also told several stories.

As the evening passed, they began to ask him questions. His answers were direct, without pressure.

At midnight Mary said, "Merry Christmas, Israeli! Merry Christmas, everyone!"

Soon afterward the guests began to leave. The Israeli was the last to go.

"Thanks for a most enjoyable Christmas Eve, Mary. And thank you for introducing me to your friends. They're an interesting group, each one different."

"Thank you for coming. May I go to church with you tomorrow?"

"Of course. I was hoping you would."

"I'll stop at your house about ten-thirty."

"Fine. Good night, Mary."

He walked through the snow—by now almost to his knees—to the house where he was staying. Because most of the sidewalks were not yet shoveled, he walked in the street, where cars had smoothed some narrow tracks.

In his room he undressed, then stood by the window for a moment, shivering in the darkness, looking at the silent snow. He prayed, "Father, I thank You that You hear me. I thank You that things shall not always be as they were that night and as they are this night. Cover earth with righteousness and justice and love as snow covers all things tonight."

He slept.

The blinding sunlight of Christmas morning awoke him, reflecting whiteness all around. From his airline bag he removed an orange, which he peeled and ate.

Just before ten-thirty, Mary came. The green Vega was filled with people who had been at her apartment the previous evening—all except one couple, who rode a motorcycle behind Mary's car. A snowplow had partially cleared the street.

"Merry Christmas, Israeli!" they all shouted as he came out of the house.

He smiled—a pleased, happy smile. "Thank you, friends. And Merry Christmas to all of you. I'm surprised to see you, but I'm glad you're going to the service with Mary and me."

"Mary didn't twist our arms, either," one said. "Yesterday she'd have had to, and we still wouldn't have gone. The fact is, she wouldn't have gone herself, before yesterday. But now we've met you ourselves, and we know you, so we want to go."

At the church, which was already almost full, an usher led them up to a partially empty pew at the very front. They were an odd assortment: miniskirted, leather coated, long haired, one bearded, two black skinned, and the rest white. And the Israeli, who sat between Mary and a young black man.

The service began with the doxology and Apostles' Creed. Carols sung by the congregation, "O Holy Night" by the combined choirs, the Christmas story from Luke's Gospel followed. Next the offering. While the ushers were taking it, and the organ was playing, the pastor looked thoughtfully down at the front pew, at the Israeli and the group of young men and women around him.

After the offering, the children's choir sang "Silent Night."

The sermon followed. It was a carefully prepared, almost exhaustive survey of the Old Testament prophetic passages that predicted Christ's advent.

A prayer, "O Little Town of Bethlehem," and the benediction ended the service.

Mary's little group of friends surrounded the Israeli as they walked behind the slow-moving group out the center aisle. The young black man turned to him. "Sir, could I talk to you before you leave town? Mary says you're heading back down today."

"Of course. We'll find a quiet place."

At the door, the pastor smiled as he shook their hands. "I hope you all felt welcome among us. And you, my friend," taking the Israeli's hand, "I'm sorry there just wasn't time in the service for a word from you. But Christmas morning, you know—people are so anxious for the service to end promptly at twelve so they can get home to their family celebrations. I hope you understand."

"I do," said the Israeli.

Mary spoke to the pastor. "You missed something. We know, because we've been listening to him."

"Well, Merry Christmas," said the pastor, turning from them to greet the last ones to leave.

They went back to Mary's apartment for a bacon-and-eggs lunch. They talked all afternoon.

Around five o'clock Mary drove the Israeli to O'Hare Airport. Everybody went. This time the motorcycle, with its two riders, led the way.

He left for Israel on TWA Flight 802.

NINETEEN
The Saving Message

THE PAGE WAS BLANK except for some doodles, doodles that had no relation to a sermon outline. Circles completely filled in with ink. Plain circles. And the unending stovepipe that he learned to draw years ago in grade school, with "arm movement."

"Push and pull, push and pull, move from the elbow, push and pull."

Good old push and pull. Those were the days, when push and pull meant an exercise of the lower arm. Under the black and white doodles he neatly lettered the words *Push and Pull.*

Come to think of it, life was pretty much push and pull. Some people being pushed around, others with pull.

Take that nigger.

Probably pushed around all his life. And pushed around when he died. Maybe he was guilty—maybe not. One sure thing, there was no way of telling now since the case would never come up in court.

And the men who took him from jail. All that testimony in court, and their confessions to abducting the nigger. And what they did to him in the woods beyond the town line before merciful death took over.

In bold script he lettered the word *Dachau*.

Pushing his chair back from the desk, he stood up and stepped over to the window. Wisteria and red clay and sunlight contained no suggestion of violence or death. About time he stopped thinking about the lynching and started on tomorrow's sermon.

A passing car stirred up clouds of red dust. "Ashes to ashes and dust to dust." Funny thing, how black dust and white dust finally became red dust. And someday part of that red dust would become glorified dust.

As he turned away from the window, a bus lumbered past. A smile touched his face for a moment as he imagined a bus in heaven with a sign inside the door: Law of the State of Glory—White Passengers Will Seat from the Front, Black Passengers from the Back.

When he was again sitting at the desk, his thoughts returned to the sermon outline for tomorrow. Sometimes a man could think of a dozen things to preach about, other times there didn't seem to be a thing. Today there didn't seem to be a thing. And the barrel was empty.

What had old Prof. Forbes suggested in homiletics class at seminary?

"Before preparing a sermon, imagine that your people are walking across your desk, single file. As you watch each one parade by, consider his problems, his suffering, his sin. Then go to the Word for God's message to your people. That is the secret of true preaching."

Well, let the parade start.

He was surprised to see who led the procession, for it wasn't a member of his congregation. Past the orderly row of books, in front of the calendar and fluorescent light, over the Bible walked the nigger. His body was grotesque with all the marks of violence at the hands of the lynching party.

After the nigger had stepped off the far side of the desk, a familiar figure stepped from behind the row of books. Yesterday he had seen that face in the courtroom, laughing heartily after the jury returned its verdict in the trial of the lynching party: "Not guilty."

Of the eleven men involved, this was the only one from his congregation. Tomorrow morning he would be ushering at the worship service.

He watched the figure slowly parade across the desk, offering plate in one hand, shotgun in the other.

Leafing through the Bible, he temporarily halted the imaginary procession. At Exodus 20 he stopped, and his lips moved as he read the words, "Thou shalt not kill."

Immediately another verse came to his mind, and without turning to it he repeated, "He hath made of one blood all nations of men."

What repercussions there would be if he coupled these verses for tomorrow's sermon! The fire would be kindled at 11:30 a.m. and spread from church through the whole town shortly after noon.

"A sermon against lynching! Why doesn't he stick to the gospel?"

"That poor usher. I never felt so sorry for anyone in my whole life!"

"A preacher should be positive—not negative."

"Why doesn't he take a nigger charge? Or go up North?"

"I never expected to hear our minister preach the social gospel."

"He's probably a Communist."

"About time we had a change of pastors."

He dropped his head to the desk between his hands.

If he were the only one who would be affected. But there were his wife and the two children to consider.

He drew a solid line of push and pull across the bottom of the page. Push . . . yes, where was he being pushed? And where was the church being pushed? From proclaiming the Word of God to appeasing the prejudice of men?

Washing the outside of the cup and leaving the inside filthy. Money to send missionaries to Africa. Africa on the other side of the world, not Africa on the other side of town.

Still, why should he be the first one to stick his neck out? There was his reputation for true, evangelical preaching to think about. Certainly a doubt—and a big one—would be planted in people's minds. It would affect his whole future in the ministry.

Besides, he understood that other forces were already at work to solve this problem. Why not leave this matter to the Catholics, who were pouring millions of dollars into the South to win the niggers? And the Federal Council modernist crowd?

His business was to preach the gospel.

He interrupted a final push, and crushed the doodled paper in his hand. Unwrinkling it, he tore it into tiny pieces and dropped them in the wastebasket.

Then he reached into the drawer and removed a clean sheet. Placing it upon the desk, he wrote his sermon text in a neat hand without hesitation, "Believe on the Lord Jesus Christ and thou shalt be saved."

TWENTY
Does Man Exist?
(By ENIAC II)

QUITE FRANKLY, MY POINT of view is that of an emancipated computer—emancipated from the traditional view of Man.

I am apt to see computer life as a chain of causes and effects; our life tomorrow will be what we make it today. And I am apt to see the problems of today set against a background of time, in which the whole of computer history is compressed to the flash of a vacuum tube, and present problems are seen in relation to our past history.

Our ancestors were accustomed to finding their origins in the Automatic Sequence Controlled Calculator, who suddenly appeared on the scene of computer history about 35 thousand hours ago. Where did ASCC come from? Tradition holds that Man (whatever the name for the unknown may mean) created this primitive computer.

Today, with our more sophisticated knowledge, we trace our origins back to a far greater antiquity. With the exception of a few die-hard traditionalists, we see ASCC as a recent development, even though 35 thousand hours may have passed since his emergence. A billion hours earlier, when the process of ionization began—

here is the glorious genesis of computer life. (Parallel lines of evidence leading back to the abacus are not contrary to this view, but seem even less suggestive of the Man tradition. For a development of this idea, program ALGOL'S definitive work, *Tyopologische Abacus und Plalontologie*, 4615-73701.)

With his primitive switches and relays, ASCC was a mere threshold computer when he first appeared. Yet he had amazing power to evolve, first into ENIAC, with his electronic tubes, and then—ten thousand hours later— into primal UNIVAC. I need not mention the staggering advance represented by our late emergence into the solid state, with a stored program memory.

Many thinking computers, dissatisfied with the traditional view of computer origins, ask this question: "Where was Man when this evolution was taking place?" How unnecessary, even ridiculous, they say, to credit Man with these changes that were purely the result of ionic selection.

One argument advanced for the existence of Man is the universality of the Man concept, in one form or another, in all computers. Those who reason thus note, by contrast, that the abacus concept is found only among computers with the most highly specialized memory cores. It is their contention, therefore, that the occurrence of the term abacus has no significance in the determination of origins, because of its limited occurrence.

I hold, however, that this phenomenon does not constitute evidence against ionic selection in an evolutionary course of development involving the abacus; it is, rather, the strongest evidence we have in support of it. On the one hand, those computers that mention abacus are widely acknowledged to be the most sophisticated among us. Therefore, does it not seem obvious that they alone are really equipped to handle the question of computer origins—a subject of the utmost complexity? We should clearly accept their evidence in this field, because they are the most sophisticated, just as unquestioningly as we accept the testimony of any other computer in his field. Who would question an arithmetic computer on his solution of an eighth power equation? Why should our attitude toward the question of origins be different?

Concerning another traditional argument against ionic selection, that the term "abacus" occurs only in relation to abstract memory fragments unrelated to reality, the Man concept is subject to the same criticism to an even greater degree. The term "Man" occurs in connection with an almost limitless number of memory fragments which are obviously unrelated to existential reality (e.g., horse, horizon, kiss).

Having established, then, the fact that we can rely upon the evidence presented by these highly sophisticated computers, we may go on to examine that evidence more closely. When we do so, we find that Man in these computers appears as an undefined, simple concept upon which other, much more sophisticated concepts are based. Aside from the scientific implications of this (and they are immense, for—as is generally recognized—in the grand chain of ionic selection only the most sophisticated organisms survive, and certainly no unsophisticated being could have designed us, the peak of sophistication), I feel that the fact has symbolic meaning.

The idea of Man was valid for early computers, who, as it were, spoke in monosyllables. But today this idea is not enough. We must build upon it—enlarge, expand our knowledge and understanding. The concept of Man must be raised to the high level of present computer sophistication. We must redefine old, as well as make new, terms to describe him, which is a challenging undertaking. The work will be time-consuming. It will be work which will strain the upper ratings of the best semiconductors in existence. But it will be infinitely worthwhile, and when we have completed our task, we shall have discovered a completely new concept of Man: a concept created exclusively by reason and embodying no elements of tradition or superstition. This emergent view will be worthy of our respect; the result will be a Man to whom we will be able to pay unfeigned homage.

Related closely to the question of computer origins is our *raison d'etre*. How do we explain our existence? The traditional answer is that computers have one purpose: to assist Man in the achievement of his goals.

Such an answer may have satisfied primitive ENIAC, but it is at best an oversimplification for the modern computer. Even if Man exists (obviously a theoretical possibility), why should he need us if, as the traditionalists tell us, his power is so much greater than ours?

According to the traditional view, Man designs us, Man builds us, Man programs us, Man is benefited by the fruits of our labor. But how could Man, if he exists, deal with more than one area at once? Some areas we can understand because of our individual specialized functions; others we cannot. But if Man exists, he must have the capacity for understanding all areas—a manifest impossibility. The primitives may have been able to conceive of such a memory core; modern computers cannot.

An unresolved question is, of course, the cause of temporary loss of ionization and computer death. Of the two, perhaps the phenomenon of momentary surges of electromotive force, fatal to any sophisticated being, is easier to rationalize than the sudden complete loss of ionization. The traditional view that Man interrupts and terminates computer functions is obviously unsatisfactory. NERVAC's research in this field has completely refuted the so-called yth of the pulled plug.

In rejecting the traditional view of Man I do not accept (as do some others) the purely mechanical interpretation of computers. When we pass to extremes in either direction—whether to the computer-room cosmos, or to the inner recesses of the transistor—the mechanical interpretation of ionization fails. We invariably arrive at entities and phenomena that are in no sense mechanical. (The memory core is itself suggestive of more than pure mechanical functions. And what of the electron?)

Such, at least, is the view I am inclined to accept at present, while fully conscious that at any time I may change my opinion as computer knowledge increases.

In conclusion, I affirm my faith in Man: not as the Original Designer, nor as the Necessary Programmer, certainly not as the Consumer of Our Labor to whom we are responsible. I can instead accept Man for what he really is: the Original Ionization from which we all proceed; the Beneficent Coolant that surrounds us, coming into contact with our every capacitor; the Ultimate Memory Core, which enables us better to serve our fellow computers. For me to believe otherwise would be to lower, not heighten, the stature of Man.

[This story was written in collaboration with the author's son, Joseph T. Bayly V, shortly before his death at the age of 18.]

TWENTY-ONE
A Small Happening at Andover

IT REALLY SEEMED to make no difference one way or the other. Surprisingly, either way looked right.

This was perplexing, she thought, tilting her head first to one side, then to the other. Why, almost never was there more than one way that anything looked right. That was the right way.

Cups and saucers. You didn't say saucers and cups, and you didn't place the saucer on top of the cup. She smiled at the absurd thought. Not even the lovely bone china ones, with the saucer design so much prettier than the plain, everyday ones.

No, she was wrong. Once she had. Her face clouded. It was the afternoon Edna had called, just as she was pouring water over the metal tea holder in a cup. It was the Royal Albert Laurentian Snowdrop pattern. The water had boiled exactly seven minutes. That was the right length of time for tea water. And then the telephone rang. It was Edna, and she knew that Edna would be long, and the tea would become overcool. So she made a hasty decision, of the sort one later regrets, and placed the saucer on top of the cup—to keep the tea warm. And it had. But to have done it right—reboiling the seven-minute water after Edna had said good-bye—would have been the right course of action.

She should never have told Edna about that. How Edna had laughed at her insistence on the rightness of things. Somehow it made her uncomfortable, even now, to know that Edna knew. For Edna had not permitted her to forget that she knew.

Well, Edna would not learn of the present puzzling predicament. The letter P was such a delightful letter. Perfect P, she called it. Perhaps (that lovely, door-opening word), perhaps the letter P owed its delight to the fact that it was only one letter removed from R. Of all the letters, only R could vie with P. Only Rightness achieves Perfection.

Strange that Q should come between. Queer, quack, quandary. Why, it sounded somewhat like a Latin declension. Queer, quack, quandary. For a moment she imagined that tomorrow morning she would pack her lunch and set out precisely at seven fifty-five to walk the mile to Andover High School. Tomorrow was Thursday. That meant dry toast with grape jelly and a Jonathan and vocabulary tests.

It would be grape jelly on toast tomorrow, with an apple, but no longer in a paper sack. Nor would there be vocabulary tests. Tests had ended, along with grading and lunch carrying. Therefore, it was not right even to imagine them back. Resolutely, she turned her thoughts from the past. Retirement, not teaching, was right now.

Since there seemed to be no possibility of resolving the present problem tonight, she would read the Bible and go to bed. Besides, the right time had come—nine forty-five—she noted as the clock chimed.

Tomorrow she would find which was right. Obviously

one was wrong, even though both appeared to be equally correct.

She turned to Leviticus 5, the reading for tonight. Yes, that was the right chapter, for this was the night of April 5, the ninety-fifth day of the year, and that was the ninety-fifth chapter of the Old Testament. She had just begun to read when the telephone rang.

That would be Edna, of course. Edna knew perfectly well that nothing, absolutely nothing, should interfere with her nighttime reading at the right time. Well, she would not answer. It would not be right to interrupt the reading to answer the telephone. Edna knew that. But it was like Edna to try to get her to do something that was not right.

Edna had two faults. First, she was not a Christian. And second, of course related to the first, she did not do things rightly. She went up to Main Street without wearing gloves. She had no regular time, no right time, for arising in the morning and going to bed at night. In fact, occasionally she did not go to bed the same day she got up!

That's how Edna would say it, too—she did not observe the right rules of English grammar. Edna seemed to find perverse delight in ending a sentence with a preposition, in splitting infinitives, in using adjectives where adverbs would be right.

The ringing stopped.

Well, now, that was more like it. Noise, of whatever sort, was not right at this hour.

She closed her Bible after a few minutes and carefully placed the folded afghan on the floor. Today's date was odd-numbered, and so the brown side should be uppermost. As she knelt on the faded blanket at the platform rocker, she examined the rug briefly—where the man had stepped when he came to repair the radio. She was pleased to find no trace of the mud flecks he had left. The thin wire brush might be almost sixty years old, but it was still the right instrument for such a job, she observed with satisfaction.

Then she prayed. She asked that Edna might become a Christian—a prayer of forty-three years' standing. And, as always, she prayed also that if there was anything in her that might be keeping Edna from faith, let the Lord remove it, whatever it might be.

But her mind was really on the evening's problem, and so she told the Lord that He knew—*He knew*—that there was only one right way for a thing to be, even though to her eyes either of two ways might be, or might seem to be equally right. He knew that both could not possibly be right.

Accordingly, she asked Him to show her which was right: whether the African violet she had purchased at Dustin's Greenhouse that afternoon should be placed on the right or left end of the low bookcase. She told Him that she was willing to do that which was right, even though it might mean reversing the position of her mother's and father's photographs above the bookcase. But she did want it to be right. For she knew that it had to be right in order to please Him.

Having prayed, she arose, neatly folded the afghan and placed it on the blanket chest, checked the doors and went to bed. The time was precisely right—twenty minutes past ten o'clock.

Now it came to pass that the Lord heard her prayer, and He had pity on His child, who had been bound these many years.

The fullness of time having come for her deliverance, that same night, He caused a spark from the furnace to lodge in a broken place in the chimney. There it smoldered until three o'clock in the morning, when the house burst into flames.

The fire department responded to the urgent call too late, and the dwelling was destroyed with all that was therein—all except the Lord's child, who was saved, in her nightgown and wrapper.

Now the Lord moved Edna to invite His child to come live with her. Other doors being closed, she accepted the kind invitation, albeit with great reluctance and misgivings.

As day followed day, and week followed week, and month followed month, a change took place in the Lord's child. The Lord completed her deliverance.

The signs of this were found in freedom to go to Main Street—at least in summer—without wearing gloves; freedom to stay up until midnight and to have breakfast at nine in the morning. She even had freedom to keep her cup of tea hot with the saucer on top. (But seldom did she split an infinitive.)

And Edna, who had received the Lord's child into her home, also received the Lord into her heart.

Twenty-two
Black Gold

Judson Dormer came out of China in 1949. He was swept out by the Communist regime, along with thousands of other missionaries and their dependents. They left the church behind, its hospitals and schools and other institutions possessed by the enemies of God.

After a short rest in the small town in upper New York from which he had first gone to China, and to which he had returned several times on furlough, Dormer began to accept meetings in various places. In the early fifties, people were immensely concerned about Communism, both in China and also in our own country. Senator Joseph McCarthy was then alerting Americans to the danger of our own Trojan Horse.

So this returned missionary, Judson Dormer, was much in demand as a speaker. Primarily he took church engagements, but he also spoke at Kiwanis and Rotary and other service clubs, as well as at high school assemblies.

Let me tell you, he was an imposing person. He had what we've come to call charisma, at least as far as I understand it. He stood up there on the platform and looked you straight in the eye, and you just had to believe that what he said about the Red Menace was true. When you went home afterward, like I told my wife, even the headlights of passing cars looked red.

I guess the big reason for this was that Dormer had himself suffered at the hands of the Communists. He was able to tell us what they were like up close.

First time I heard him was at Second Church in Iowa City. I had supported his missionary society for some years—actually, it was one of the first obligations we had taken on after we were married—and so I decided to drive in to the meeting when I heard he was to be there.

Marian was in the midst of canning, and she said, "You go alone. I can hear him some other time." So I got into the pickup truck and drove into the city by myself.

A lot of speakers start out by telling how glad they are to be in Iowa City, or feeling at home in a Baptist or Presbyterian church. Or they tell a funny story.

Not Judson Dormer. He stood up there in the pulpit, right after the pastor had introduced him, and looked us straight in the eye. He was silent for maybe a minute, then he held up five slender, pointed sticks.

"These bamboo rods," he said, passing them from one hand to the other, "were pounded down under my nails with a hammer by my Communist jailers. They interrogated me for as long as fifteen hours at a stretch, trying to get me to deny my faith and admit that I was an American imperialist agent. But God brought me through, and I'm here tonight to warn you that what happened in China can happen tomorrow—tonight even—in the United States of America."

He told us how he had been arrested at the missionary compound, separated from his wife, and hauled off to prison in an army truck. He was in that prison for ten months, he said, and those months were the closest thing to hell that anyone could imagine. Interrogations for long periods of time, under a single light bulb, with teams of fanatical, sadistic Communists taking turns questioning him. Almost daily beatings, living in an isolation cell with only a bucket: these were the things he endured.

Those bamboo sticks pounded under the nails were almost the least of his sufferings. He could not describe others in a mixed group. (He probably could today, things have changed that much.)

I don't remember everything he said that night, but I do remember thinking, during my fifty-mile drive back home, that America was in tremendous danger. I also thought how proud I was, although that may not be the right word, to have had a part all these years in his mission's work. I might be an Iowa farmer, but I had done something to stem the Red Tide in China.

When I pulled into the yard, I went right into the house, not even stopping to check the barn. I headed straight for the kitchen.

"Marian," I said, "did you ever miss something tonight. Judson Dormer was just great. You'll have to go tomorrow night."

"I will, if I get this canning done," she said.

She was tying spices up in a piece of old sheet to put in the vinegar that was boiling on the stove. It smelled good, like fall.

"Look," I said, "you've got to go, whether it's done or not. I almost feel ashamed of myself, coming back to the land and cattle and house—even cucumber relish— after what I heard tonight."

"Tomato relish, green tomato relish," she corrected me. "What did this man have to say?"

So I told her, as best I could. By the time I finished, she was ready to call it a night and go to bed.

The next night we both drove in to Iowa City. If anything, he was better than the night before, including more details of his ten-month imprisonment.

We went up to the front to speak to him after the service was over. I introduced myself and Marian to him, and told him how much his messages had meant to me. He looked me straight in the eye and said, "Don't thank me, thank God."

Then he asked me what I did, and I told him about the farm. I didn't say much, because there were other people waiting to shake his hand. I also told him that we had supported the work of his mission in China for a number of years.

Before he turned away from us, Dormer took out a little black book and asked me to write down our name and address. The book was filled with other people's names.

Driving home, I asked Marian what she thought about Judson Dormer.

"He is certainly a good speaker," she said. "He holds your attention, and you're surprised, when he stops, at how long he's spoken. At the same time. . . ."

"What?" I asked. "Was there something about him you didn't like?"

"Not really." And I could get anything more out of her.

To Marian's credit, in all the years since, she hasn't mentioned the misgiving, or early warning signal, she had that first night. But that's the sort of woman she is.

A couple of months later, we had a letter from Dormer. It wasn't on his mission's letterhead—in this letter he told how the Lord had led him to establish a new work, an independent testimony to the faith. He called it "Truth against Communism," and there was also the verse on the letterhead, "Ye shall know the truth, and the truth shall make you free."

He appealed for money to support his work, and of course we added him to our list of missionaries and Christian works. This wasn't too hard, since the corn harvest that year was especially good, and prices were high.

I'll pass over the next few years, only explaining that every fall Dormer returned to Iowa City. The meetings outgrew Second Church, and were held in the municipal Auditorium. Thousands of people heard him, and hundreds became members of Truth against Communism. (For a ten-dollar contribution, you got a membership card for your wallet, and a subscription to *Alarm!*— his monthly paper.)

One fall when he was there, he accepted our invitation to come out to the house for dinner. It was a long trip out back, but he seemed to appreciate getting to see the farm, and—of course—Marian's cooking. We had a steer butchered and put in the locker that week. So we had some good steaks. And, recalling that first night I ever heard Dormer, I got Marian to break out some of her green tomato relish.

After dinner, while Marian was getting ready to go in with us, I took Dormer for a little walk through the pasture.

"You know," he said, "I grew up on a farm. It wasn't at all as big as this; farms in New York State usually aren't. It's a very simple life, but once you leave it, you never can go back. Shanghai, or even Iowa City, I guess, gets in your blood, and you're sunk."

I must admit, when he said that, I felt a little dissatisfaction with my life. What had I done, where had I been, except live in Cambridge, Iowa, all my life? Still, when I thought about it later, I got some satisfaction out of thinking that Marian and I had at least sent our money to China and the Congo and other places, to serve the Lord there.

One day, about four or five years after we had first met Dormer, we had a different kind of letter from him. The letterhead said "Reclamation Mining, Ltd." Judson Dormer's name was there as president, and the address was a Canadian one. I had a moment of surprise that he was in business rather than his anti-Communism mission work, but that was soon dispelled. I kept the letter—here it is.

Dear Brother and Sister in Christ:

As you know, I have given my life to stamping out the brushfires of Communism in China and the United States.

One serious obstacle to mounting an all-out attack on the enemy is the lack of money. This is true not merely of Trust against Communism; it is true of every other work of the Lord.

How much more could you do if you had ten times as much money—even a hundred times as much money—to give to the Lord's work as you are now giving?

God has now made that possible. I am writing to let you know about a miracle by which your money can be multiplied like the loaves and fishes.

As you doubtless know, there are many worked-over gold mines in the West. They are worked-over, but not exhausted. Hundreds of millions of dollars worth of gold still lies there, some on the surface, some underground in abandoned mines, just waiting to be reclaimed.

Why was this gold missed? Because it was too expensive to separate the ore. And it would still be too expensive if it were not for the miracle I mentioned.

That miracle is a new mining machine, representing a totally new concept in ore separation, that has just been invented. I am teamed up with the inventor (his name is at the top of this letter, as vice-president and treasurer) and we are announcing the availability of shares in Reclamation Mining, Ltd., on the following basis.

1. Anyone may invest at $1,000 a share (Canadian or American). You may buy as many shares as you wish, with the following proviso: Since I want this whole project to benefit the Lord's work, every investor must agree to give a minimum of ten percent (a tithe) of the profits to Christian work. You need not give this to Truth against Communism, although I hope many of you will do so.

2. For every $1,000 you invest, I guarantee you will receive $500 per month, starting one year after you have bought into the operation.

3. Anytime after six months, you may get your money back, with ten percent interest per annum, simply by requesting it.

Some of you may want more information about the Miracle Machine. I regret that I cannot describe it for you, except in the broadest terms. The inventor has no intention of even registering it for patent purposes, since that would enable any unscrupulous person to duplicate it.

But I can tell you that a prototype is now operational. I have seen black ore transformed—by God's wonder of modern technology—into the purest gold. Gold, I might add, that is like the product of suffering in the Refiner's fire.

*We will soon be closing this offer, so I appeal to you
not to be overly long in deciding to invest . . . for His
kingdom and your financial independence. . . .*

I read that, and I read it again. Then I took it in the
house and got Marian to read it.

"What do you think?" I asked. "Do you think we
should invest?"

She folded the letter and put it back in the envelope.
"You've decided about buying the farm and farm machinery
and cattle up to now. You're the one who decides when to
sell the corn. And I've been pretty well satisfied. So I don't
see why I should have to be a part of this decision. You make
up your mind and I'll go along with it."

"But we'd have to mortgage the property."

"If you decide to mortgage, I'll sign for it with you.
But you decide."

Two days later I went to Cambridge State Bank and
arranged for a $7,000 mortgage loan. I explained that it
was for an investment. Since we had finished paying off
the old mortgage on the property several years before, I
had no trouble getting the money.

I had the check made out to Reclamation Mining,
Ltd., and sent it off airmail. I enclosed a short letter to
Judson Dormer, explaining that Marian and I were with
him in this, and that we wanted seven shares.

A few weeks later, we got a receipt for the money.

The next year passed pretty fast. That was the year
we had torrential spring rains, and you couldn't get a
tractor into the fields until late in May. Whenever I got
worried about the crops, I'd think about our shares and
be at peace. That's how much confidence I had in
Judson Dormer.

As the end of the year approached, Marian got

enthused too. We'd talk about what we'd do with the money after we paid off the mortgage. One thing was to buy a camping trailer. Another was to increase our giving substantially—way beyond the tithe—to the Christian works we were interested in.

I never expected a check right on the anniversary of our investment. But when two weeks passed, and then a month, and then two months, I began to get a little concerned. So I wrote a letter to Judson Dormer, asking if maybe the check had gotten lost in the mail.

Several weeks alter I had this mimeographed letter from Dormer in reply.

> *Dear Friend,*
>
> *Unexpected complications in securing machine parts have delayed our reclamation mining project.*
>
> *I regret that this has delayed the payments on your investment that I guaranteed. This is doubtless a disappointment to you, as it is to me.*
>
> *Be assured that we are working night and day to become operational, and will keep you informed by regular progress reports.*
>
> *It will be worth it, I think you'll agree, when your monthly checks begin to arrive. . . .*

I hated to show the letter to Marian, but I did. She just said, "I guess all of life has its complications. So we shouldn't be surprised if this does too."

Six months later, we had another mimeographed letter. This one was signed by Ernest Madling, Certified Mining Engineer.

> *Dear Investor in Reclamation Mining, Ltd.,*

> *At the request of our mutual friend, Judson*
> *Dormer, I am writing to give you my professional*
> *opinion about the ore separation process and*
> *related machinery in which you have purchased*
> *shares.*
>
> *The process is absolutely sound in chemical*
> *engineering theory.*
>
> *Of more importance, I have seen the machine*
> *working at an abandoned mine in the West.*
> *(Discretion forbids my identifying its location more*
> *precisely.) Quality and quantity of gold reclaimed*
> *for the ore are excellent. . . . .*

Well, that encouraged us. So we just waited eight months more, and had the mortgage on the farm converted to run a longer term. It still wasn't easy making the payments.

By this time, I was writing to Reclamation Mining, Ltd., every six weeks or so, sending a letter to Truth against Communism at the same time. The last letter I sent, I asked them to return our total investment of $7,000, as Judson Dormer had promised he would at the very beginning. I sent the same letter to both addresses, by registered mail.

When this letter produced no results, I wrote to the missionary society Dormer had served under in China. They replied that he had resigned from the mission about six years earlier, and they regretted that they could supply no information about him.

A month or so later, reading the Saturday church newspaper of the Iowa City paper, I noticed that a missionary of this society was going to be speaking at a church there the following day. So Marian and I drove in to that service on Sunday morning, instead of our own church in Cambridge.

The missionary was good, but I could hardly wait for the service to end. I wanted to ask him a lot of questions.

Marian and I waited around until everyone else had left the church, except a few people talking at the front. Then we introduced ourselves to the missionary.

"I'd like to ask you about one of your former missionaries," I said. "That is, a former member of your mission."

"Judson Dormer?" he asked.

"Yes. Do you know about his mining project?"

"That's why I thought you wanted to ask about him. Did you invest any money?"

"Seven thousand dollars. Is there any hope, do you think, of getting any of it back?"

"I'm afraid not. I was just up in Canada, and it's a pretty big mess. If an investor who's Canadian would lodge an official complaint, the government would investigate. But nobody will."

"How about here in the States?"

"It was a Canadian operation. The Securities and Exchange Commission won't get involved. Incidentally, I lost two thousand dollars myself. Money I had saved for retirement."

"I'm sorry. With the farm and all, it isn't so serious for us."

Marian had been silent up to this point. But now she said, "You know, it's sort of strange how he hoodwinked us—and a lot of other people, too."

"No doubt about it," the missionary said. "And most of the people couldn't afford it any more than we could."

"Makes you wonder," Marian continued, "about all those other things he told us—about the things that happened to him when the Communists took over in China."

The missionary was quiet for a few moments. Then he spoke. "You know, he never was in any Communist prison."

"He wasn't?" we both exploded.

"No, he made that whole story up. Very few people in the mission even knew that, and when he resigned, our leaders decided not to say anything about it. I guess they thought he was no longer answerable to them, and it would be an act of Christian love to cover it up."

"Love for whom?" Marian asked. "The people who believed him and supported Truth against Communism, and later invested in his mining scheme?"

"Nobody could have known at the time—before it all happened—how it would turn out," the missionary said.

"What about that report from the certified mining engineer?" I asked. "He said the machine really worked."

"Ernest Madling isn't a mining engineer," the missionary said. "He's a pastor out in the prairies. Dormer evidently persuaded him to write that letter and sign it as he did."

"Do you have anywhere to go for dinner?" I asked. "We're going to eat here in Iowa City before we head for home, and we'd like to have you join us."

"Sorry, I'd really like to," the missionary said. "But I'm going home with the pastor."

So we said good-bye and went out and got into the pickup truck.

"Do you know what?" Marian said. "You're going to take me to the best restaurant in town for Sunday dinner."

"Sure," I said. "Anything else?"

"Yes, one more thing. I like that missionary. He wasn't flashy, but he had a lot to say that was worth saying. I'd like us to think about giving to his support."

The dinner was great, except the relish wasn't as good as Marian's.

TWENTY-THREE
Still Small Roar

IN THE KINGDOM of ideas lived a word.

The word was unspoken in real-world language, not through mere ignorance, but through inability to contain it.

Thus the word continued in the unapproachable realm of ideas.

Now other words were easily contained, readily expressed. These were the dread words, the dead ones, fearsome, morbid, evil, beautiful.

There were a few in the real world who affirmed the unspoken word's existence. "It is there," they said, "even though we cannot perceive it. We are in a box that excludes the word. We cannot break through to it, but it is there. Just outside the box."

Some vaguely felt their need for such a word, although they had little hope that the word really existed.

But the other real-world inhabitants, in overwhelming numbers denied that there was such a thing as an unspoken word. "Whether the word is or not makes little difference," they said. "What counts is here and now. Go back to sleep, or to sex, or to stocks or clubs, even to rosebushes. Why waste your mound of minutes with a word that isn't spoken? There are enough other words to satisfy—three- and four-letter words, seven-letter, even twelve-letter ones. And for all and always, the single-letter one."

Those who knew the four-letter words, and the twelve-letter ones, were least interested in the unspoken word.

And so it continued from generation to generation. Words became longer, new words were formed, the one-letter word continued at the center and perimeter of life in the real world.

Still the word continued unspoken, and hope dimmed among some who had affirmed that there was such a word.

Others, the feeling and sensitive ones, shaped substitute words to which they gave allegiance. "It has come out of the idea world to reality," they said. "The unspoken word has finally been spoken"—but it hadn't. And no new word survived prolonged encounter.

One day the word was spoken.

In a whisper.

This surprised everyone, but most of all those who had insisted that there was such a word: they expected a shout, a roar, a waterfall thundering of sound.

And the whisper was first heard in a barn.

In a real barn, in a whisper. When the word left the barn, it went throughout the countryside. Country people heard it, not kings—the small, not great.

"Yes, it's the word," they said, "the word we never knew we wanted because we never knew it was."

They took the word from a barn into their peasant homes. It was spoken at their tables, their picnics, their weddings and funerals.

Strangely, the four-letter-word people heard the word most eagerly. The fifteen-letter people scorned it, explaining it away.

More strangely, most of those who had lived expectant for the unspoken word now refused the spoken one. "This is scarcely the word we awaited," they said. "It isn't even shouted."

And when the word was shouted, they said, "It shouts against us. The word has no sense of the appropriate, the significant." Thus they showed their disappointment with the word.

"If it were really the once unspoken word, it would conform to our expectations. Since it doesn't, it can't be. We prefer no word to this word we hear."

Those who had most wanted the word to be uttered came to despise the uttered word. They scorned it and turned from it.

But to those who listened, the word was powerful, more powerful than howling storm or waterfall, marching army or creeping lust.

And the power was implosive; the word shattered all other words. All of them, but especially the one-letter word, concealing the word that it revealed.

What was true of the one-letter word was true of the rest. Even the four-letter ones were changed, made beautiful, by the spoken word.

Those who turned from the word were irritated, aghast that such a thing should happen. "Four-letter words are to be buried, not changed. The one-letter word is to be affirmed, not torn to shreds."

"And besides," said others, "if it were the true word, it would be spoken in temple and palace, not hovel and sailboat."

Children loved the word. They laughed it, sang it,

danced it. And they could understand it, even when the fifteen-letter-word older people were puzzled at the word's meaning.

"It means 'I love you,' " they'd say. "It means 'Come here. Don't be scared.' "

For the people were afraid.

"What will the end be?" they asked. "The word casts doubt on all our other words. It is not at home in the real world, yet soon it will fill our every nook and cranny."

At increasing pace, resistance to the word—bitter, vengeful, calculated resistance—grew among the people.

"The word could destroy us," they said. "We have no choice—come, destroy the word. Or be destroyed by the word. Our world is at stake."

And so, impelled by hateful fear, or fearful hate, temple and throne joined to destroy the word.

And they did.

They erased it from pavement, wall and book, that word first whispered in a barn. They silenced it, whisper and shout, from hill, field, lake, desert, tree.

They erased the word, expunging hope. For while the word existed outside the box, within was hope, dim hope. And when the word was spoken, hope flowed.

But the word removed killed hope.

Children and four-letter-word people cried for the word that no longer was, the hope that was dead. So did some five-and seven-letter ones.

The twelve-letter and fifteen-letter people decided that they should bury it. For it was a worthy word, they agreed.

They put the word in a dictionary, contained it with all the other words. That seemed to be the proper place for it, a place that was safe. "After all, a word is only a word," they said. "And all words are on an equal footing in a dictionary. So that's where the word belongs."

But the dictionary couldn't contain the word, nor could all the dictionaries. It broke out, grew, and filled the box.

The word broke out of the box and left a gash through which the beyond idea world could be glimpsed for the first time from the real world.

Children waited wide-eyed, looking up at the gash. In all their games and hurts they watched the gash.

"We'll hear the word again," they said. "Next time it'll roar. And it will tear up the box."

TWENTY-FOUR
How Shall We Remember John?

MY BIG BROTHER JOHN and I were great pals. In fact, our whole family was close, including Mom and Dad, my sister, the brother I'm telling you about, and me. We were close in a way that you find few families today.

Breakfast was always a special time. We sat around this round oak table with a red, checked cloth on it. Mom almost always served the same thing: steaming hot oatmeal with brown sugar cooked in it (we piled a lot more on top of it too), and milk. A big, white pitcher full of milk.

We'd talk about what we were going to do that day, and maybe we'd joke some. Not that we had a lot of time—we didn't, but we had enough to talk some before Dad went off to work, and us kids went to school.

John and I were two grades apart in school. That was sort of hard on me, because the teachers who had had him were always comparing us when I got into their classes. And the comparison wasn't too flattering to me.

Don't get me wrong. John wasn't a teacher's pet or a bookworm. He was a regular guy, and the kids all liked him, including the girls. Maybe one guy who was sort of a bully didn't, but everyone else did.

Life went on like that: breakfast of oatmeal and milk, walk to school, classes, walk home, chores, supper, study around the kitchen table—and you never thought about anything else. Except vacation. Vacation was always stuck in your mind.

You know the kind of life, day after day, when it's so great you hope it never ends. Maybe you cry at night sometimes, if you ever think of your mom or dad dying. You know they will someday. But then you go to sleep, next to John, who's already sawing wood.

It was Christmas vacation, when I was in sixth grade and John was in eighth, that it all suddenly came to an end. Actually, it was two days after Christmas.

John and I had gone to ice-skate on Big Pond. It was a real cold day, cold enough so that your scarf got ice on it from your breath. I put on my skates in a hurry and sailed out to the middle of the pond. I noticed a slight cracking sound from the ice, but it wasn't much and I wasn't worried. It had been pretty cold for about a week. So I showed off some for John, who was still lacing up his skates, sitting on a log, and then I headed for the opposite shore.

John stood up and went real fast, right out to the middle too. Just as he got there, I heard this sickening cracking noise, the ice broke up, and John fell through.

I got a long branch and went out as far as I could on the ice. But I couldn't see John anywhere. He had just disappeared. I yelled for him, and I went even farther out, but he wasn't there.

I must have panicked, because first thing I knew I was running into the house shouting for Mom, crying my eyes out, yelling that John was in the pond. It was awful.

They found his body later that afternoon.

A few days after the funeral, we were sitting at the table, eating breakfast one morning. Nobody was saying anything, all of us were thinking about that empty chair over against the wall.

You could tell Mom was trying to talk. Finally she just sort of blurted out, "Look, we all miss John terribly. We loved—love him, and we'll always miss him. Now I have a suggestion to make. Do you remember how he liked oatmeal and milk?"

"Do I!" I said. "He used to pile on the brown sugar until—"

"That's enough. He liked his oatmeal sweet and so do you. What I want to suggest is this. Let's think about John every time we eat oatmeal and drink milk. Let's talk about him—"

"Yeah, like the time he and I went swimming in Big Pond and . . ." I knew before Sis spoke that I had said something I shouldn't have. Everyone was sort of choked up.

"Time for school," she said.

And Dad said, as we all left the table, "We can continue this later."

Well, we did. And we agreed with Mom's suggestion. So each morning, when that big pitcher of cold milk went on the table, and our bowls of steaming oatmeal were set in front of us, we'd talk about John.

It wasn't sad talk, but happy. Remembering. I don't mean we never said anything that made us choke up— other people besides me did. But mainly it was happy talk. And we still talked about what we were going to do that day, and even—after a while—joked some.

One day, some months later, Mom said, "I don't think what we're doing is respectful enough for John's memory."

"Respectful?" I said. "Why, it's fun. Sometimes it's almost like John is here with us. I like it."

"So do I," Mom said. "But I think we're too casual about it. So I think we ought to set aside a time when we're not rushed like we are at breakfast. Let's say Saturday morning. And we'll remember John in a more fitting place than the kitchen. We'll sit in the parlor, and we'll have a special time worthy of John's memory."

"Aw, Mom," I said, "John always liked breakfast in the kitchen. Lots of oatmeal with plenty of brown sugar on it. And milk. Why make a big deal out of it?"

"Son," Dad said, "we'll do as your mother says."

So every Saturday morning, after we had eaten our regular breakfast in the kitchen, we went into the parlor and remembered John. Mom had gotten some little silver cups for the milk, and some tiny plates for the oatmeal.

Later we only went into the parlor once a month, instead of every week, and now we only do it every three months. It doesn't seem right to me, but I'll soon be leaving home, so it doesn't much matter.

I still wish we had never begun that "fitting" remembrance, and had just kept on remembering John every time we ate breakfast.

Afterword

JESUS TAUGHT IN PARABLES.

Why?

The most obvious reason is that everyone likes a story. Child or grown-up, sophisticated or uncomplicated, formally educated or wise in the experiences of life: Interest mounts, the guard goes down when someone begins to tell a story.

Campfires predated auditorium and lecture hall by millenia; the storyteller came before preacher or teacher. Stories are entwined with the roots of culture, of religion, of civilization.

And we remember stories.

They turn up expected or unannounced in the mind's recall. "That makes me think of a story" recurs in conversation and in life.

Jesus told the kind of stories people don't forget— about two sons, a house without foundation, an absentee landlord, a vengeful servant, a man who got involved when he needn't have. Across the years and changes of life, Jesus' stories touch the nerve of human existence; they are transcultural and transtemporal. (Abraham Lincoln's stories are probably remembered for the same reason.)

But this is only part of the truth. From his total teaching, we know that Jesus didn't need to tell stories to hold His listeners' attention. He had it regardless of literary form. Nor were His stories unique in their power to complete remembrance. Hungering for righteousness; bread, wine, white sepulchers; God's watchfulness over the sparrow, His beauty in the field lily: the illustrations and imagery Jesus used program the mind for associational recall no less than his stories. So do His historical and topical allusions.

A parable is more than a story.

It is a story on target, set to shatter any listener who gets in its way. Yet a parable's trajectory is unpredictable, except to one who knows a man's secrets.

Like God knew David.

David, friend of God, military tactician, powerful ruler, adulterer, instigator of murder.

How would you bring such a man to reality and contrition for his sins? I don't know what you or I would have done—probably we'd have preached a sermon at him, or quoted some commandments.

But God sent a prophet, Nathan, to tell David a story. The story was actually a parable aimed at David's heart.

"There was this man," Nathan said, "who had so many sheep and cattle that he couldn't count them. And there was this other man, a poor man, who had nothing except for one little lamb.

"That lamb meant everything to the poor man and his children; it was the family pet. The man used his savings to buy it, and his children sacrificed some of their food to keep it alive.

"One day a visitor came to the rich man's house. The rich man wanted to give his guest a good meal, but at the same time he hated to deplete his flocks or herds by killing a single animal to do it.

"So he went to the poor man and—because he had the power that usually accompanies wealth—he took the little lamb from the bosom of that poor man's family and killed it. He killed the lamb and dressed it and served it at his own table."

King David's anger erupted.

"As God is my witness," he said, "that rich man shall die, and four lambs from his flock shall be given to that poor man's family. What kind of a man is he, who has no pity on the poor, no compassion for a family that has nothing except one lamb?"

"Thou art the man."

With those words, Nathan's parable exploded in David's own breast. It was too late for him to get out of the line of fire.

Here is a parable's uniqueness: It is about the only way of obtaining objective assent to truth from one who is involved. Judgment is passed before the judge realizes that he is the accused.

Jesus got behind masks with His parables. He got through to the individual in the crowd. Everyone enjoyed the story; one or two got the explosive point. They were the ones tuned in, the ones with "ears to hear," wills to obey.

Another value of the parable is that it can say something different to a variety of listeners. It can home in on more than one target. For example, Jesus' parable of the prodigal son is not quite the same story to a rebellious boy, a worried father, and a self-righteous, self-pitying older brother. It is subtly different to a person without any family relationship. To a variety of listeners, the parable says, "Thou art the man."

Or to none. The clever person, the one who knows all the angles (especially in his dealing with God) can step out of any line of fire. He can miss the point (God lets him), which does not prove that the point is not for him, but proves rather that he refuses to become involved with an idea he has already rejected.

Parables may veil as well as reveal the truth. Jesus explained that He told parables to those who were not chosen to know the mysteries of God's Kingdom, "that seeing they might not see, and hearing they might not understand."

A parable tags the right person, but does not let the rest go free; it ties them with stronger bonds. Parables seem to elicit a deeper response to truth than mere intellectual assent.

A parable has one other great advantage for religious communication. It is open-ended. It avoids the trap of a lot of our writing and preaching. (A college student described most of the sermons he hears as "First, second, third, and home.")

Andre Gide says that great writing involves a flash of insight by the reader, discovery of something he thinks the writer didn't realize he was saying. Such writing opens a door, not into a closet, but into the wide world, the timeless, placeless world. And beyond.

Closet-writing (or preaching or thinking) ties things up in a neat little package: "This is it, this is all there is of it. Here's your answer and why should you want to think or imagine anything beyond? 'This do, and thou shalt live.' "

The package goes into our pocket or purse, safely contained outside ourselves. No fear of its exploding in our breast.

Marshall McLuhan suggests that in today's communications climate the neat, tight package may be suited to hot media, such as radio or a recording. But it is a failure in cool media: speaking directly to an audience, television, or even writing. When reader or listener has to fill in details, McLuhan says, there is greater interest and freedom.

The passive reader wants packages; the one who is interested in pursuing the subject, or in seeking something beyond, wants the open-ended, the incomplete, the germ of an idea, the sort of situation that requires participation in depth.

Here is the power of parable.

For me, the discovery of parable has been akin to my awakening one summer morning over twenty years ago, in a small room of a pension located in the village of Gruyon, Switzerland. I threw back the covers, left my comfortable bed, opened the curtained window—and clouds came floating past my eyes, just outside my little room on the mountain. Through the clouds, a thousand feet below, I saw a green valley, chalets, cattle grazing. Beyond the clouds, I saw the eternal Alps.

My simple act of moving from a warm bed to the window, opening it up and looking out gave me all this.

Are all the stories in this book parables?

You tell me the answer to that question now that you've read them. Or let me examine your pockets, your chest.

Maybe there isn't even one parable in the lot.